# THE BEST OF MELBOURNE

T0357989

# THE BEST OF
# Melbourne

# Contents

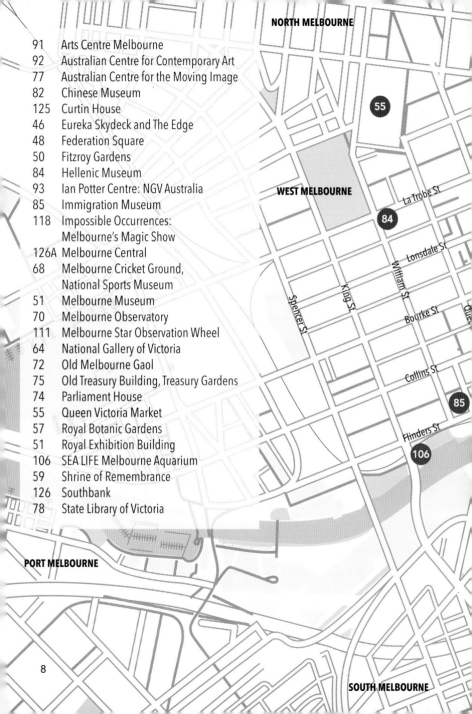

NORTH MELBOURNE

WEST MELBOURNE

PORT MELBOURNE

SOUTH MELBOURNE

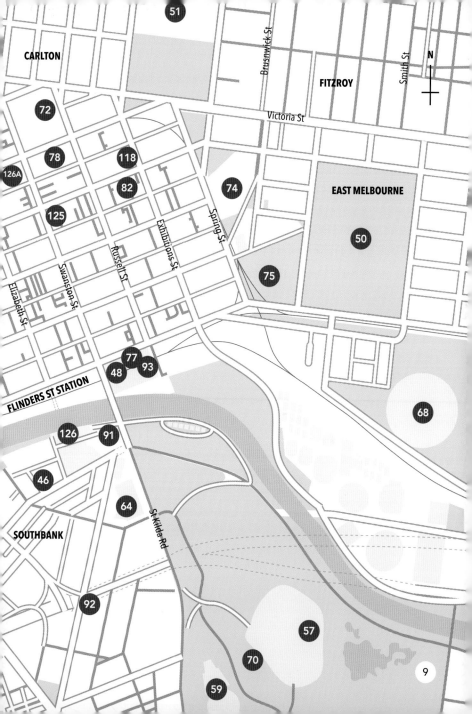

CARLTON

FITZROY

Brunswick St

Smith St

N

Victoria St

72

78

118

126A

82

74

EAST MELBOURNE

125

Spring St

50

Exhibitions St

75

Russell St

Swanston St

Elizabeth St

77

48

93

FLINDERS ST STATION

68

126

91

46

64

SOUTHBANK

St Kilda Rd

92

57

70

9

59

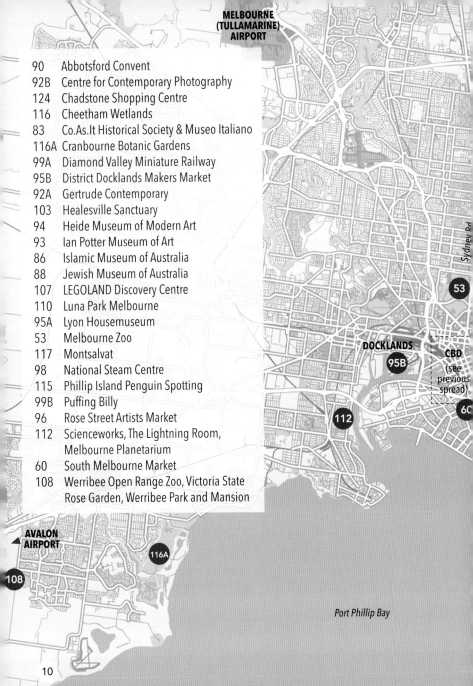

MELBOURNE
(TULLAMARINE)
AIRPORT

Sydney Rd

53

DOCKLANDS

95B

CBD
(see
previous
spread)

60

112

AVALON
AIRPORT

108

116A

Port Phillip Bay

# Welcome to Victoria

Victoria is Australia's smallest mainland state. At 237,659 square kilometers, or 91,761 square miles, it's about the size of Romania and only slightly smaller than the United Kingdom, which gives you some idea of how much land the UK gave up when Australia became an independent nation in 1901. True to Australia's reality of being one of the least densely populated countries in the world, the total population of Victoria is only about 6.5 million – less than one tenth that of the UK. So even though Victoria has, by far, the highest population density of any state in Australia, it's only dense by Australian standards. Like practically everywhere else in Australia, there's plenty of wiggle room, unless you're looking for a parking spot in inner-city Melbourne on a Friday or Saturday night.

Victoria is bordered to the west by South Australia and to the north by New South Wales. The northern border follows the squiggly course of the Murray River from the South Australian border to where the Murray actually starts, before making a south-east beeline to the coast. To the south of Victoria is the Tasman Sea, separating Victoria from Tasmania, about 330 kilometers (205 miles) further south.

Victoria has a varied climate, ranging from cold, semi-arid in the north-west to warm summer Mediterranean in the south-west to predominantly oceanic. Translated into plain English this means that for the most part the climate of Victoria is very similar to that of New Zealand, France, the United Kingdom and Ireland. Australia likes to promote itself as a warm country of endless, yellow-sanded beaches but Victoria is cooler and wetter than most of Australia, and

it really is a lot more like much of western Europe; still gorgeous, but not surf, sand and bikini gorgeous – more winery and alpine gorgeous.

Victoria's climate and rainfall lend themselves to agriculture and more than half the state is devoted to agricultural production. Wheat, barley and oats are the main grains. Victoria produces a third of all of Australia's apples, almost all its pears and a hefty portion of its stone fruits. Tomatoes, potatoes, carrots and broccoli are major vegetable crops. Close to 20 million sheep and their lambs graze Victorian grasslands, so there are three sheep to every person. Victoria is almost literally Australia's land of milk and honey. Almost one-third of all Australian beekeepers live in Victoria and the state accounts for a whopping two-thirds of the nation's milk.

# Welcome to Melbourne!

No other state capital dominates its state like Melbourne dominates Victoria (with the exception of Canberra, but that's another story, and the Australian Capital Territory isn't a state anyway).

Melbourne is home to 75 per cent of all Victorians. Defining the size of a city can be tricky. At 2080 square kilometers (803 square miles), the City of Melbourne is Australia's geographically largest city, but even this figure is dwarfed by Greater Melbourne, which comprises 9992 square kilometers (3858 square miles), making Greater Melbourne larger than New York, larger than Cyprus and larger than about 20 other countries.

This town of five million people – Australia's second largest, and only *slightly* smaller than Sydney – began its life a little fitfully. On 26 January 1788, Captain Arthur Phillip and the First Fleet established a settlement at Port Jackson in Sydney. This predominantly penal

colony, in spite of early teething problems and a shaky start, turned out to be somewhat of a success, so the powers that be back in England decided to start other colonies. In October 1803, Colonel David Collins and the passengers and crew of the HMS *Calcutta* started a colony at Sullivan Bay, near the present-day township of Sorrento, at the southern extreme of what is now Greater Melbourne. The colony struggled because Collins was stuck with people he couldn't trust, and he never got accurate information on the locale. After 7 months, 21 convict escapes and 30 deaths, Collins was given permission to abandon the site. They relocated to Risdon Cove in Van Diemen's Land, now a town 7 kilometers (4.3 miles) north of Hobart, the capital of Tasmania. Collins later became the first Lieutenant Governor of the Van Diemen's Land colony and the founder of Hobart. One of the main streets of downtown Melbourne, Collins Street, and a smaller street, Little Collins Street, are named after him. There's a Collins Street in Hobart too. Barely a trace of the Sullivan Bay colony exists today, and it would be a generation before another settlement was attempted in what was then still the southern extreme of New South Wales.

Fast forward to May 1835. Businessman, grazier, entrepeneur-ahead-of-his-time, and Van Demonian, John Batman, decided that maybe, just maybe, the land around Port Phillip Bay might not be so bad after all and it might be a fine idea to found a colony there. Batman crossed the Tasman and made contact with the elders of the Indigenous Wurundjeri. Somehow, he managed to strike a deal with them and the result was Batman's Treaty – essentially a land purchase deal in exchange for tribute. The importance of Batman's treaty is unappreciated even by most Australians. It remains the first and *only* time Europeans negotiated a settlement deal with

EVERYDAY
IN EVERYWAY
RAISINS

19

the traditional owners of the land and it formed the basis of the establishment of the idea of owners of native title.

Of course, stupidity had to enter the picture and Batman's desire to acknowledge traditional title conflicted with colonial policy, turning the whole foundation of Melbourne into a bit of a mess.

But to cut a long story short, effectively what happened is that Europeans led by pioneer John Fawkner started settling the area around the Yarra River on 30 August 1835, with Batman's group arriving on 2 September. Melbourne's foundation day remains officially 30 August. Batman wanted to call the settlement Batmania.

Fortunately, that name didn't have a hope and by March 1837 the place was officially named Melbourne, after William Lamb, 2nd Viscount Melbourne, the Prime Minister of the UK at the time. The area that would be known as Victoria remained part of New South Wales until 1851, after which it became a colony in its own right.

Batman and his family settled at what would later become known as Batman's Hill, at the western end of Collins Street, where today stands a blue post to mark the spot, in a park next to a railway line. The area is being redeveloped into a commercial office precinct called Collins Square. Batman was to die only four years later in 1839 at age 38, crippled and disfigured by syphilis, estranged from his wife but cared for by the local Aborigines. His only son, aged about nine, drowned in the Yarra River on 11 January 1845. Batman's wife and seven daughters, however, survived. Batman's legacy remains mixed. His neighbor in Van Diemen's Land, artist John Glover, described him as 'a rogue, thief, cheat and liar, a murderer of blacks and the vilest man I have ever known.' Please don't hold back, Mr Glover, tell us what you *really* thought.

Almost 200 years on, Melbourne has come a long way from a scraggly collection of huts and cattle pens. Melbourne is, much as Sydney might hate to admit it, the cultural capital of Australia. Of all Australian cities it is the one that has most unashamedly renounced 'the great outdoors' image that Australia so loves to cultivate. It has, instead, fully embraced 'the great indoors', most probably because the weather can be, shall we say, 'challenging'.

## Dressing for Melbourne's Weather

Days in a Melbourne summer can make you think, 'This is just lovely' and then later make you feel like you're living in a blast furnace. Although the average high is about 20° Celsius in the year (a reasonable 70° Fahrenheit), the highest temperature each year is generally over 40° Celsius (an unreasonable 105° Fahrenheit).

Melbourne winters can be icy. It's easy to forget that the southern coast of Australia is the last continental land until you reach Antarctica. The average yearly low is about 11° Celsius (50 degrees Fahrenheit) with the lowest temperature somewhere around freezing. The last major snowfall was in 1951 and Melbourne's suburbs haven't had snow since 1956, but that doesn't mean that global warming has kicked in permanently. Melbourne weather can always surprise you, and often does.

Even Melbournians never quite get used to the weather. It's quite conceivable that, in any season, but especially in spring and summer, in the same day you can be roasting *and* freezing, that you'll need an umbrella *and* find that an umbrella is unnecessary.

Anyway, rain is different in Melbourne. It's seldom large, heavy, drops like you'll find in Brisbane, Hobart and Sydney. Melbourne rain is often a light, genteel rain, which in the colder months can turn into frosts and fog.

Melbourne's famously cantankerous 'four seasons in one day' weather results from it being, at 37° South, perilously close to the roaring forties. This is a zone of the Southern Hemisphere where a combination of air displaced from the equator and moving towards the south pole, the earth's west-to-east rotation, and a lack of breaking land masses, create strong westerly winds and instabilities that make the weather a challenge to dress for.

So how do you dress for Melbourne's weather? The secret is layering. Multiple layers of thinner clothing are more versatile than fewer layers of thick clothing when the weather is highly variable.

And take the weather report with a grain of salt! As wonderfully accurate as they can be for other parts of the country, Melbourne weather has a mind of its own and almost seems to take pleasure in making meteorologists look like fools.

## The People of Melbourne

Humans have been living in the Melbourne, Yarra River Valley region for at least 40,000 years. The Yarra River is about 242 kilometers (150 miles) long and is a perennial river – not all parts flow all-year round. This is somewhat ironic, since the term 'Yarro-yarro' in the Boonwurrung language of the Wurundjeri people means 'always flowing'. However, by the time it reaches the Melbourne metropolitan area, where the Wurundjeri, Boonwurrung and Wathaurong lived, it is a continuous, rather silty flow. The river's *real* name is *Birrarung* – 'River of Mists' – far more accurate and poetic.

Since 1835 Melbourne has gone through several demographic shifts. Early data is unreliable, but it's possible that there were never more than a couple of thousand Indigenous inhabitants living there, and even then occupation wasn't continual (the weather, remember).

After the Aboriginal peoples were more or less pushed out by Europeans, Melbourne gradually entered its 'patrician phase'. Then the discovery of gold in Victoria in the 1850s created a gold rush. Melbourne's population bloomed and there was suddenly a lot of

money about, turning Melbourne into a financial center, the world's richest city (for a time) and the focus of a long land boom. Within a generation new money became old money and Melbourne became the center of Australia's 'establishment'.

When Australia became an independent nation on 1 January 1901, Melbourne became Australia's capital city, a reality that Sydney only agreed to because Sydneysiders knew that the condition was only temporary until the foundation of Canberra in 1913 – although the capital wouldn't really shift until 1927, when Canberra was actually *built*.

Post-World War II, Melbourne, along with the rest of Australia, experienced massive immigration from war-torn Europe. This gave the city an injection of cosmopolitan verve which persists to this day. By the early twenty-first century almost 40 per cent of Melbourne's population was born outside of Australia – among them significant Chinese, Italian and Indian populations.

Of special note is the Greek population of Melbourne. For many years there were more urban Greeks in Melbourne than anywhere else in the world outside of Athens and even today it still has the largest Greek-speaking population outside of Europe. Now that Greek Australians are in their fifth generation, almost half of all Greek speakers in Australia live in Melbourne.

This confluence of nations and cultures is a significant factor in Melbourne's special flavor.

## Melbourne's Personality

Melbourne is a city of wide streets, boulevards and avenues, except in the center where it's a fascinating complex of small streets and lanes with all sorts of treasures waiting to be discovered by the persistent visitor who's prepared to do a lot of walking.

It's an eclectic city, with a vibrant cafe and restaurant culture. Melburnians visit more cafes per capita than anyone else in Australia – almost two-thirds of the population are regular cafe customers. But they don't win this statistic by much with Hobart and Sydney close behind.

As mentioned before, the weather plays a substantial role in Melbourne's continuing cultural development. Because the outdoors is so, well, *problematic*, creative people flock to Melbourne to exchange art and ideas in the great indoors. The city is funky and edgy in an East Village New York, Bethnal Green London, with a touch of Barcelona, sort of way. And it's a city with a sense of humor, the center of Australian comedy.

And, so, in spite of its drawbacks – and there are some – it's also among the world's most functional cities and is *still* considered one of the world's leading livable cities.

You'd think that with so many cultural influences that Melbourne would be a city with an identity problem, but nothing could be further from the truth. The city definitely has its own thing going. If Melbourne were a person she'd be the zany, eccentric aunt of the family. She's the sophisticated woman-of-the-world bohemian who wore tie-dyed dresses in the 60s and who now looks like a rich gypsy. She's the funny, grand old dame with the raucous laugh that the more straitlaced members of the family roll their eyes at while secretly, desperately, wishing they had her freedom.

## What Melbourne Has That Other Places Don't Have

Unlike so many cities that caved in to pressure from the automobile industry in the early years of the twentieth century, Melbourne never got rid of its **trams** (page 35) and they're still a major part of its public transport system. The Melbourne Tram Network, with 24 routes covering 250 kilometers (155 miles) is currently the largest in the world – and Melburnians make full use of it.

The city is truly a wonderful place to **shop** (pages 121–27), especially for **clothing**. Many of its cafes serve all-day breakfasts, which are a fun way to eat.

Melbourne is a relatively flat city, making it easy for bicycling, and the city authorities have gone to rather a lot of trouble to install bike

lanes and other measures to encourage biking.

It's a city that likes to laugh and has more **comedy clubs** than any other city by a long stretch (pages 118–20).

It's a dog-friendly and child-friendly city too. There are plenty of places to take the **kids** (page 97) including the famous **Puffing Billy Locomotive** (page 99), and, if you're there in early March, The **Moomba Festival** (page 130).

Melbourne is football mad. The natives are particularly fascinated by Australian (Aussie) Rules Football, administered by the Australian Football League (AFL), and the AFL Grand Final is so important that the Friday before the Saturday game is a state holiday. And, of course, there's the **Melbourne Cup** (page 132). There's a state holiday for that too.

# Melbourne Street Names and Suburb Boundaries

One of the more confusing aspects of Melbourne is that, for historical reasons, the names of streets change when suburbs change. Another complication is that main streets are often the boundaries of suburbs. So, for example, Elizabeth Street Melbourne becomes Royal Parade when it hits Parkville to the north, but if you go further north still the west side of Royal Parade is in Parkville but the east side is in Carlton North and then the road becomes Sydney Road when it hits Brunswick further north again. This might be fine for the locals, who are used to all this, but it can be crazy making if you're trying to identify an exact address, so if you occasionally see multiple street names and suburbs in the directions you'll know why. Don't say we didn't warn you.

## Getting Around

Getting to Melbourne is as easy as getting to any other Australian capital city. Perhaps easier. It's serviced by no fewer than four airports: Tullamarine, in the city's outskirts, is the city's principal international airport. Avalon Airport is further west and services the city of Geelong too. Essendon Airport was Melbourne's principal airport up until 1970. It is the most centrally located of the airports and now focuses on cargo, charters and regional services. Moorabbin Airport services the south-east.

Trains will take you to Adelaide, Canberra and Sydney and a trans-Tasman ferry will take you to Davenport on Tasmania's north coast.

Once you're in Melbourne, if you have your own car you'll find that it's easy to get around and parking, while sometimes not so easy, isn't impossible. The public transport system is one of the best in the country, especially for a visitor.

## Public Transport

Public Transport Victoria (PTV) is the company that coordinates public transport for not only Melbourne, but all of Victoria. It's an integrated network of trains, buses and, of course, trams. For geographical reasons, **ferries** (pages 38–39) don't play a crucial role in Melbourne, in spite of the size of Port Phillip Bay, and you're unlikely to be catching one unless you plan to explore the south-west and south-east of Greater Melbourne, but they are fun, nevertheless.

For the purposes of simplicity, all directions to Melbourne attractions will be from **Flinders Street Railway Station**, right in the heart of the Melbourne Central Business District (CBD). Downloadable maps of the train and tram networks can be found at **www.ptv.vic.gov.au/more/maps**.

Melbourne buses can get rather complicated, so PTV suggests that you use their online journey planner: **www.ptv.vic.gov.au/journey**.

## Planning Your Trips

If you have access to the internet the online Journey Planner is relatively easy to use: **www.ptv.vic.gov.au/journey** or if you're techno-minded, download the app from your preferred app store. However, if you're a luddite and technology is just a little too confusing, then call 1800 800 007, and if you need help planning your journey, select option 2. Customer service is open from 6.00 am to 12.00 am daily and all night Friday and Saturday.

On the whole the Melbourne public transport system is very user friendly. Being a multicultural city means that they are very aware of the challenges faced by people whose first language is not English. You can find information in other languages here: **www.ptv.vic.gov.au/footer/customer-service/information-in-other-languages** or you can call 03 9321 5450. Hearing impaired TTY users can call 03 9619 2727. Overseas customers can call +61 3 9662 2505.

## Paying for Public Transport – The Myki Card

If you're travelling on public transport by train or coach in regional Victoria, you can get away with a paper ticket. But if you're in metropolitan Melbourne you *have* to have a Myki card to pay for your transport. Fortunately, the Myki system is very easy to use.

## Step One: Buy your card

You can buy a physical Myki card at:

- Hundreds of different newsagents, shops and all 7-Eleven convenience stores
- Many railway stations
- Online
- Pre-ordering by calling 1800 800 007 (PTV will mail you your card) For details go to: **www.ptv.vic.gov.au/tickets/myki/ buy-a-myki-and-top-up/where-to-buy-and-top-up**.

The cost of a Myki Card is $6 for adults and $3 for concessions, seniors and children aged 5 to 18. Myki cards are FREE if you're a Victorian pensioner or Victorian Senior Card Holder. Children under four travel FREE and don't need a card. There are also a number of provisions for eligible students.

If you have an Android phone you can also get a Mobile Myki as an app extension to Google Pay. You'll need to be aged 16 and over to use Google Pay and you'll need to link your Mobile Myki to a Visa or Mastercard. Details at **www.ptv.vic.gov.au/ tickets/myki/mobile-myki**.

## Step Two: Register Your Card

Depending on how you buy your card you can either register your card or not. PTV strongly recommends registering your card because if it gets lost or stolen you effectively lose your travel credit. However, if the card is registered you can call 1800 800 007 and immediately cancel the card, order a new one and all credit can be transferred from the lost card to your new one. Also note that a Myki card expires after four years and registered users are contacted to buy a new one if needed.

## Step Three: Top Up Your Card

Your Myki Card needs to have money credited to it. You can do this manually at most places where you buy the card, either in person or using a machine. You can also arrange for auto top-up so that if the balance falls below a certain amount the card gets credited by an amount that you nominate. Since topping up can take anything up to 90 minutes and something can always go wrong we recommend that for full fares you set the top-up to when the minimum balance falls below $20 and the top-up is also $20, that way you'll always know that there's enough money on the card. Use half those amounts for concession cards.

## Step 4: Using your Card

Using the Myki is easy. Just tap the card onto the scanner at your train station, on your train, on your bus and on your tram before boarding. On alighting, tap off.

Public transport in Victoria is very reasonably priced and has a daily cap at $8.80 for full fare or $4.40 for concession and other fares.

## Free Trams in Melbourne

Melbourne trams are a fun way to get around the city and you can pay for them with your Myki. But the truly great news is that PTV has made tram travel within the central CBD of Melbourne totally FREE. Just hop on and off to your heart's content and as long as you begin and end your journey within the Free Tram Zone you don't need a Myki.

Pick up a map at the **Melbourne Visitor Hub** (page 40) or at **www.onlymelbourne.com.au/free-tram-zone**.

As a further bonus there's Route 35, the FREE tourist tram, which is a charming, old tram that's still in service after almost a hundred years. Route 35 takes you right around the perimeter of Melbourne's CBD with a short leg into **Docklands**. The route runs both clockwise and anticlockwise around the city center, bounded by Spring Street and Nicholson Street in the east, La Trobe Street in the north, a diversion into Docklands Drive in the north-west then Harbour Esplanade in the west and the length of Flinders Street in the south. For a map of Route 35, go to **www.ptv.vic.gov.au/route/1112/35**.

## Melbourne's Night Network

On Friday and Saturday nights there's a need for additional train, tram, bus and coach services, especially when taxis and Uber rides become scarce, and even more so because drink-driving penalties in Australia are among the strictest in the world. Thus, the need for Melbourne's Night Network.

For further Information go to **www.ptv.vic.gov.au/more/travelling-on-the-network/night-network** but here's a quick summary:

### *Night Trains*

After 1.00 am the city circle stations close and all trains from the city depart from Flinders Street Station. Night Trains run at least every 60 minutes on almost all lines with additional shuttle trains

on the extended network. All services pick up passengers in both directions so you can actually start you night late, or your morning early. For safety, premium stations are staffed all night.

## Night Trams

Routes 19, 67, 7, 86, 96 and 109 run every 30 minutes.

## Night Buses

There are 21 Night Bus routes, and they connect with trains at suburban stations. They run every 30 to 60 minutes. There are special designated Night Bus stops and you can get on or off at curbside tram spots and any bus stops along the route. If in doubt, ask your driver.

# Melbourne Ferries

In the event that you do want to experience Melbourne Ferries and explore some of the watery outer fringes of Melbourne you have four options: Geelong and Port Phillip, Western Port and Westgate Punt. They are a very nice way to travel, especially in the warmer months.

Please note that none of Melbourne's ferries are integrated into the Myki system, so you purchase your tickets on board.

For timetables and further information go to **www.ptv.vic.gov.au/more/travelling-on-the-network/ferries**.

Please note that if you're planning a trip via ferry it might be better to call PTV directly on **1800 800 007** and speak to a human being because the trip planner website is pretty useless in this regard.

## *The Port Phillip Ferry*

Operates between Victoria Harbour in Docklands and runs services to Geelong or to Portarlington on the Bellarine Peninsula. For timetables, bookings and further information go to **www.portphillipferries.com.au** or call **03 9514 8959**.

## *The Western Port Ferry*

Operates between Stony Point on the Mornington Peninsula then to French Island and then to Cowes on Phillip Island. For timetables, bookings and further information go to **www.westernportferries.com.au** or call **03 5257 4565**.

### The Westgate Punt

The Westgate Punt ferry is a short-hop route that crosses the Yarra between Westgate Landing at Fisherman's Bend, near Westgate Park at the extreme west of Port Melbourne, and The Punt, which is a short walk to **Scienceworks**, the **Lightning Room** and the **Melbourne Planetarium** (page 112) in Spotswood. The fare is $2.70 each way on weekdays and $5 each way on weekends. Weekend service is on demand ('you turn up, we take you across'). For the weekday timetable go to **www.westgatepunt.com** or call **0419 999 458**.

## Going Your Own Way

If you want to go your own way there are a number of rent-a-car companies and yes, Melbourne also has Uber services. Melbourne is a city with a highly developed infrastructure and services, but you'll still have problems getting a cab on a Friday or Saturday night if you don't book ahead.

### Melbourne Taxi Cab Numbers

| | |
|---|---|
| Australia Wide Taxis | 131 008 |
| 13cabs | 132 227 |
| London Taxis | 131 001 |
| Silver Top Taxi | 135 000 |
| Silver Service Melbourne | 03 9088 0786 |

To get a ballpark figure on how much a taxi will cost go to **www.taxifare.com.au/rates/australia/melbourne.**

Many cab companies offer minibus services if you need to book a cab for more than four people. Maxi taxis are taxis large enough to accommodate up to 13 people and are about 20 per cent more expensive than normal taxis because they always charge peak rate. Some specialist, more luxurious taxis, like London Taxis, always charge at the peak rate but many people are happy to pay the extra because they are roomier.

**Wheelchair accessible taxis** must be booked ahead, call **1300 133 320** or **0404 990 115**.

In Australia, it is considered polite for at least one passenger to sit up front with the driver, unless you're only traveling as a couple. It's part of our tradition of egalitarianism, which we still pay a lot of lip service to.

## Tourist Information

Melbourne Tourist Information, aka the Melbourne Visitor Hub, is the nerve center of visitor information for Melbourne.

Address: 90–130 Swanston Street, Melbourne, 3000

Phone: +61 3 9658 9658 (Monday to Friday)

Website: **www.melbournetouristinformation.com**

How to get there: From Flinders Street Station it's a 10-minute walk north up Swanston Street, or a short, FREE, tram ride.

Opening hours: 9.00 am to 6.00 pm seven days.

OK. Are you sitting down? Because we have some weird information for you. Melbourne Tourist Information is located on the grounds of **Melbourne Town Hall**. The Town Hall offices are only open Monday to Friday, so there's no weekend telephone service. At the time of writing there is no direct telephone line to the Melbourne Visitor Hub and it is staffed by volunteers.

Anyway, the Tourist Hub is very easy to get to, and open seven days. There are also a number of smaller information booths scattered around the Melbourne CBD.

# The Melbourne Interactive Map

The City of Melbourne has developed an online interactive map that is very useful: **maps.melbourne.vic.gov.au**.

You can zoom in to quite an impressive level of detail, down to individual houses and businesses, sometimes to the level of individual trees of note, so if you have a smartphone or tablet it's pretty difficult to get lost. It includes listings such as the location of drinking fountains, chemists and the all-important public toilets. There are also listed taxi ranks and Night Network (listed on the map as Night Rider) bus stops. The map is still under development and some of the links don't work, but it's a pretty nifty tool if you invest just a little time getting acquainted with it.

Perhaps its most impressive feature is the search box. If you know the *exact* name of what you're looking for, as in the official name as listed in this guide book, and if it's in the CBD or the central suburbs (the area encompassed by the City of Melbourne jurisdiction), then you'll have little trouble finding exactly where something is. Unlike certain other online maps (which shall remain nameless) all the streets and street numbers are clearly marked and accurate.

Click on all the little red stars scattered throughout the map and read the information. You'll no doubt find something of interest.

Suburbs included in the City of Melbourne Interactive Map are:

- Carlton, Carlton North and Parkville
- Flemington and Kensington
- Melbourne, East Melbourne, West Melbourne and North Melbourne
- Port Melbourne, Docklands, South Wharf, Southbank and South Yarra.

## The Smart Way to Visit Melbourne

Every city in Australia has a list of their must-see attractions, and while what is and isn't on a list depends on who you talk to, and how long that list is, there are always a few attractions that should be on everyone's list. But after the 'must-sees' your stay in Melbourne is more a matter of 'What sort of experience are you looking for?'

Are you interested in history or art? Do you want to explore coffee, food and wine? Do you love the great outdoors? Do you want to visit places that the kids will love too? Or do you want it *all*? This book is arranged around sites and attractions that have a common theme, so that you can plan your trip accordingly.

Please Note: all opening hours of venues and attractions mentioned in this book are given in AEST (Australian Eastern Standard Time) so you can plan when to call or make bookings just in case you're holding this book in your hot little hand while outside of the Victorian time zone. All opening hours, admission prices and other costs are correct at the time of publication but are subject to change without notice so, if in doubt, telephone the venue or consult their website before committing to your plans.

# Must-sees

Centre Place, Melbourne

# Eureka Skydeck and The Edge

Why you should go: Eureka Tower is either the tallest or second tallest building in Australia, depending on how you measure it. Although mostly a residential building, the highlight for the visitor is the observation deck, the Eureka Skydeck 88, comprising the entire 88th floor and offering 360-degree, panoramic views of Melbourne. At 285 meters (1260 feet) it has the highest publicly accessible vantage point in a building in Australia.

The Edge is a glass cube that extends 10 meters (33 feet) from the building's structure and is suspended 300 meters (almost 1000 feet) above street level. The floor of The Edge becomes transparent once the cube is fully deployed.

Address: 7 Riverside Quay, Southbank 3006

Phone: 03 9693 8888

Website: **www.eurekaskydeck.com.au**

How to get there: Walk south from Flinders Street, over the Yarra River using the Evan Walker Bridge. Keep walking south along Southgate Avenue then turn right (west) along Riverside Quay. The whole walk should take you about 15 minutes. It's practically the tallest building in Australia so it's hard to miss.

Opening hours: 10.00 am to 10.00 pm seven days, last entry 9.30 pm.

Time budget: About an hour.

How much? If booking online: adults $21 adult, concessions $16.50, children $12.50, family (2 adults and 2 children) $57, family (1 adult and 2 children) $38, extra child $10. **Edge upgrade**: adults $12, concessions $10, children $8, family (2 adults and 2 children) $29, family (1 adult and 2 children) $20, extra child $6.

While you're here: If you're super keen you can go one level higher to the **Eureka 89** restaurant. Their degustation menus start from $115. You're also right in the middle of the Southbank Precinct and near the **National Gallery** (page 64).

# Federation Square

Why you should go: Located right in the heart of the city, Federation Square is a venue for major events, as well as exhibitions and smaller events that happen at a range of venues within the site. Some are permanent, some are temporary, some only happen at particular times of the year. It also has restaurants, bars and specialty stores. 'Fed Square', as the locals call it, is mostly housed in a building as spectacular as it has been controversial, but it has its enthusiasts, being considered by fans of public squares to be in the top ten in the world.

Address: Corner Flinders Street and Swanston Street, Melbourne 3000

Phone: 03 9655 1900

Website: **www.fedsquare.com**

How to get there: It's a two-minute walk from the east exit of Flinders Street Station. You can't miss it.

Opening hours: Open 24 hours a day, although individual venues, businesses and events have their own opening hours.

Time budget: At least an hour.

How much? FREE! Although venues within the square might have admission charges and other costs involved.

While you're here: You're within a stone's throw of: **The Ian Potter Centre: NGV Australia** (page 93), dedicated to Australian art, and the **Australian Centre for the Moving Image** (page 77). It's also the stepping-off point for **river cruises** (page 115) and **coach tours**. There are FREE guided tours of Federation Square that depart at 11.00 am Monday to Saturday from the Australian and Aboriginal and Torres Strait Islander flags in the Swanston Street forecourt. Bookings not required.

## Fitzroy Gardens

Located just east of the CBD, in spite of being so close to where the action is, it's not often frequented by tourists or visitors, so it's a nice little island of peace and a great place to recharge your batteries. On the grounds you'll find a number of points of interest, details of which are available on the website (**www.fitzroygardens.com**).

In particular, take note of **Captain Cooks Cottage**, which is the original English building reconstructed in Australia.

Website: **whatson.melbourne.vic.gov.au/PlacesToGo/CooksCottage/Pages/CooksCottage.aspx**; Opening hours: 9.00 am to 5.00 pm seven days; adults $6.70, concessions $5.10, children (5–15 years) $3.60, family (2 adults, 2 children) $18.50.

## Melbourne Museum and the Royal Exhibition Building

Why you should go: The Melbourne Museum houses some of Australia's best natural history collections and the gallery of taxidermy has to be seen to be believed. You'll get a lot more out of your visit if you go to the website first and take a look at the 'What's on Today' page, where you can choose the date of your visit and see exactly what's on offer.

Don't forget to visit the **Bunjilaka Aboriginal Cultural Centre** in the museum: **www.museumsvictoria.com.au/bunjilaka**.

Address: 11 Nicholson Street, Carlton 3000

Phone: 03 8341 7777

Website: **www.museumsvictoria.com.au/melbournemuseum**

How to get there: Located in the middle of Carlton Gardens, it's a huge, modern, glass-fronted building. Catch the FREE tram from Flinders Street to the corner of Victoria Street and La Trobe Street and just walk north for five minutes across Carlton Gardens.

Opening hours: 10.00 am to 5.00 pm seven days.

Time budget: At least three hours.

How much? Adults (over 16 years) $15. If you have any sort of concession that the museum accepts, then entry is FREE, although surcharges apply for special exhibitions. You might consider becoming a member (page 62).

While you're here: The museum is also home to an IMAX cinema where you can see documentaries as well as general release movies; Phone: 03 9663 5454; Website: **www.imaxmelbourne.com.au**.

The museum also has the special Pauline Gandel Children's Gallery designed as an activity space for under-fives. The museum even caters to kids on the autism spectrum. Phone for details.

Carlton Gardens are a pleasant place to stroll on a sunny day and the delights of **Brunswick Street** (page 122) are only a couple of blocks to the east. The Royal Exhibition Building, just south of the museum, is an extraordinary example of Victorian architecture and is definitely worth a look at when something is on; Phone: 131 102; Website: **www.museumsvictoria.com.au/reb**.

# Melbourne Zoo

Why you should go: Because, being close to the CBD, it's a very accessible zoo with more than 300 species on display. Although it dates back to the Victorian era, the zoo (formally know as Royal Melbourne Zoological Gardens) has been extensively modernized to keep up with our current knowledge about how to create a comfortable environment for wildlife. Highlights include Lion Gorge, the Orangutan Sanctuary, Wild Sea (showcasing Victoria's coastal and ocean life), Trail of the Elephants and the much-loved Butterfly House.

Address: Elliott Avenue, Parkville 3052

Phone: 1300 966 784

Website: **www.zoo.org.au**

How to get there: The 'fast' way (20 minutes), take a train to Royal Park Railway Station then it's a short walk. The 'scenic' route (25 minutes), take tram 59 from the corner of Elizabeth Street and Flinders Street to Royal Melbourne Hospital, then tram 58 to Zoo.

Opening hours: 9.00 am to 5.00 pm seven days.

Time budget: At least three hours but you could easily spend the whole day here.

How much? Adults (over 16 years) $37, seniors $33, concessions $28, FREE for children (4 to 15 years) on weekends, public holidays and during public school holidays, $19 for children Monday to Friday outside of holidays. You might consider becoming a member (page 62) especially if you also plan to visit **Healesville Wildlife Sanctuary** (page 103) and the **Werribee Open Range Zoo** (page 108).

While you're here: Melbourne Zoo offers an ongoing program of special exhibitions and events. Some are on all the time, like the monthly Sunday **high tea** in the Rainforest Room. Check the website to see what's on.

# Queen Victoria Market

Why you should go: Officially opened in 1878, the Queen Victoria Market is a Melbourne institution and an excellent way of watching the locals go about the business of living. Queen Victoria Market has more than 600 fresh produce stalls, cafes, restaurants and specialty shops – artists and makers but also lots of junk as well. There are special events on all the time too.

Address: Officially Queen Street, Melbourne 3000, but bounded by Peel/William, Franklin, Therry, Elizabeth and Victoria streets

Phone: 03 9320 5822

Website: **www.qvm.com.au**

How to get there: Take any of the trams that go up Elizabeth Street – routes 19, 57, 58 or 59. The five-minute trip from Franklin Street is entirely within the FREE tram zone.

Opening hours: The **Fresh Produce section** opens at 6.00 am Tuesday, and Thursday to Sunday, and closes at 2.00 pm Tuesday and Thursday, 5.00 pm Friday, 3.00 pm Saturday and

4.00 pm Sunday. Closed Monday and Wednesday but the **Winter Night Market** is open from 5.00 pm to 10.00 pm from early June to late August. **String Bean Alley** and the **Specialty Shopping** sections open at similar times to **Fresh Produce** but check the website. Other shops in the precinct are open from around 9.00 am to 5.00 pm seven days.

Time budget: At least three hours.

How much? FREE or as much as you like depending on how much the wares on offer tempt you.

While you're here: Foodies will love the two-hour **Queen Vic Market Ultimate Foodie Tour** with its 'generous tastings'. Adults $69, children (5 to 14 years) $49, under 5s free. Bookings at **www.qvm.com.au/tours**. **The Hellenic Museum** (page 84) is a short walk to the south. The other shopping delights of **Melbourne Central** (page 126) are a short walk to the south-east, which is practically next door to the **State Library of Victoria** (page 78). **Old Melbourne Gaol** (page 72) is a short walk to the east and from there it's not all that far north to the **Melbourne Museum** (page 51). See also the **South Melbourne Market** (page 60).

## Royal Botanic Gardens

Why you should go: Because it's 36 hectares (89 acres) of garden gorgeousness comprising over 8500 botanical species. Highlights include the **Tropical Glasshouse**, **Guilfoyle's Volcano** and the **Arid Garden**, the **Ian Potter Foundation Children's Garden** and the **National Herbarium of Victoria**.

Address: Officially Birdwood Avenue, South Yarra 3141, but in reality bounded by St Kilda Road, Domain Road, Anderson Street, Alexandra Avenue and Linlithgow Avenue.

Phone: 03 9252 2300 or 03 9252 2429 for the Visitor Centre open 9.00 am to 5.00 pm

Website: **www.rbg.vic.gov.au**

How to get there: Take any of the trams that go down St Kilda Road, or simply walk – it's a 15-minute, very pleasant stroll from Flinders Street until you reach the northern perimeter of the

gardens. **Alexandra Gardens** and **Queen Victoria Gardens** are at this northern perimeter. While they are not officially part of the Botanic Gardens, they are essentially an extension of this green area, and you can stroll through them on your way there.

Opening hours: 7.30 am to sunset, so closing time is extended in the warmer months.

Time budget: At least two hours.

How much? FREE, but donations are always welcome. There is also a continuous timetable of reasonably priced special events. Check the website for details and bookings. A FREE, 90-minute guided tour commences at 10.30 am, departing from the Visitor Centre. There's also a 30-minute hop-on, hop-off, minibus **Garden Explorer Tour** departing from Oak Lawn; adults $10, children and concessions $8.

While you're here: On the grounds you'll find **Government House**, which holds FREE tours of its gardens every month; Website: **governor.vic.gov.au/tours-and-open-days/government-house-garden-tours**. The House is also open for FREE intermittently a few times a year for the curious general public. Notably, on Australia Day, 26 January, but also as part of **Open House Melbourne**, a program that allows public access to almost a thousand buildings the general public usually don't get to see and that takes place on the last weekend of July. Website: **www.openhousemelbourne.org**.

The House itself is also open as part of a combined tour with historic **La Trobe's Cottage** every Monday and Thursday from 10.00 am to 12.15 pm; Phone: 03 9656 9889; Website: **www.governor.vic.gov.au/tours-and-open-days/national-trust-tours**; adults $18, concessions $13, children $10.

The **Shrine of Remembrance** (below) and **Melbourne Observatory** (page 70) are also located in the Botanic Gardens. You can go **punting on the lake** (page 104) and if you're in Melbourne in the summer, you might want to make a booking at the **Moonlight Cinema** (page 132).

If you're a real enthusiast and willing to travel, the **Botanic Gardens** also has another site located in **Cranbourne** (page 116).

## Shrine of Remembrance

Why you should go: Both a monument and a museum commemorating World War I, the Shrine is a must-see for history buffs or anyone looking for a profound emotional experience. It consistently ranks in the top-10 things to do in Victoria.

Address: Officially Birdwood Avenue, South Yarra 3141, but in reality on the grounds of the Royal Botanic Gardens

Phone: 03 9661 8100

Website: **www.shrine.org.au**

How to get there: Take any of the trams that go down St Kilda Road, or simply walk. It's a 15-minute, very pleasant walk from Flinders Street.

Opening hours: 10.00 am to 7.30 pm seven days.

Time budget: At least 90 minutes if you are doing the tour.

How much? FREE, but donations are always welcome. There is also a continuous timetable of reasonably priced special events. Check the website for details and bookings.

While you're here: A 75-minute guided tour commences at 11.00 am, and 12.45 pm departing from the **Visitor Centre**; adults $34, concessions $29, children $15, children 6 and under FREE but not recommended due to themes and content.

Combine the tour with a 'tiffin', a sort of gourmet picnic, available from the adjacent Jardin Tan restaurant. Tour and a Tiffin cost: adults $64, concessions $59, children $34. Tour and a Tiffin requires 24-hours' notice. For bookings, phone or visit **www.shrine.org.au/Visit-the-Shrine/Shrine-Tours**.

Remember that you're on the grounds of the **Royal Botanic Gardens** (page 57), with all the delights available to you there.

## South Melbourne Market

Why you should go: Because if you love markets and the **Queen Victoria Market** (page 55) isn't enough then South Melbourne Market is for you. It's less touristy than the Queen Vic and is yet another opportunity to indulge in food and other shopping while getting up close and personal with the locals. Highlights include the **Neff Market Kitchen Cooking School**, the **SO:ME Creative Trading Space** and the **Summer Night Market** on eight consecutive Thursday nights in January and February.

Address: Officially Coventry and Cecil Street, South Melbourne 3205, but also bounded by York and Ferrars Street

Phone: 03 9209 6295

Website: **www.southmelbournemarket.com.au**

How to get there: Take a tram or walk to the corner of Flinders Street and Spencer Street and then take either tram 12 that will

take you to York Street and walk west or take tram 96 to Ferrars Street and walk east. The tram driver will let you know where to get off. The whole trip should take 15–20 minutes.

Opening hours: 8.00 am to 4.00 pm Wednesday, Saturday and Sunday, 8.00 am to 5.00 pm Friday.

Time budget: At least three hours but you could easily spend the day here and in the surrounding South Melbourne shops.

How much? FREE or as much as you like depending on how much the wares on offer tempt you.

While you're here: On every third Saturday of the month, you can take a **To Market to Market Tour** from 10.00 am to 11.30 am; costs $20 and includes a market bag with food samples.

South Melbourne has a variety of specialty shops that are fun to window shop in, or you can catch tram 96 and continue your journey all the way to St Kilda and finish the day there.

# Special Deals for the Melbourne Visitor

## *Museums Victoria Membership*

Website: **www.museumsvictoria.com.au/join-support/membership**
How much? Adults $59, concessions $39, children $17,
  households $99.

Museums Victoria offers a membership deal with benefits for both the casual and frequent visitor to Melbourne, including special member-only events. But the most important benefits to even the casual Melbourne visitor are unlimited **free general entry** to Melbourne Museum, **Scienceworks** (page 112) and the **Immigration Museum** (page 85) and discounts to **Melbourne IMAX** (page 52), the **Lightning Room** (page 112) and **Melbourne Planetarium** (page 112).

There is also free entry to other great museums both interstate and internationally. For more information go to: **www.museumsvictoria.com.au/join-support/membership/signup**.

## *Zoos Victoria Annual Membership*

Website: **www.members.zoo.org.au**
How much? Adults $120.25, seniors $102, concessions $91.80,
  children $36. Paid either in full or in instalments over 12 months
If you're a great fan of animals, among other bonuses, like member-only events, this membership gives you: unlimited express entry to **Melbourne Zoo** (page 53), **Healesville Sanctuary** (page 103) and the **Werribee Open Range Zoo** (page 108). For adults, seniors and concessions and for children under four there is also FREE reciprocal entry to Sydney's Taronga Zoo and Taronga Western Plains Zoo, Adelaide Zoo, Monarto Zoo (South Australia's open-range zoo) and Perth Zoo.

## Melbourne Big Ticket Legoland and SEA LIFE Melbourne Aquarium Pass

Website: **www.melbourne.legolanddiscoverycentre.com.au/tickets/melbourne-big-ticket**

How much? $45 per person (adults over 16 years and children 3 to 15), children under 2 FREE.

**Benefits:** Visit either venue on any day and you can visit the other venue within 90 days after purchase. Legoland Discovery Centre is located in Chadstone Shopping Centre about 17 kilometers (10 miles) from SEA LIFE Melbourne. Check the Chadstone Shopping Centre website (**www.chadstone.com.au/tourist-shuttle-bus**) to book your FREE Shuttle to/from SEA LIFE Melbourne.

Conditions:

- Children under 16 must be accompanied by an adult
- You will only be able to purchase a combination ticket if a child ticket is included
- Guests visiting LEGOLAND Discovery Centre must be accompanied by a child, and guests under 16 must be accompanied by a parent or guardian aged 18+

Note: The **Merlin Annual Pass** allows you to see 11 attractions in Australia and New Zealand and represents excellent value for money even if you only plan to visit Sydney and/or Melbourne and/or Brisbane sometime in the next 12 months after purchase. For details go to **www.melbourneaquarium.com.au/tickets/merlin-annual-pass**.

From time to time the pass even goes on sale, which means even more savings. Annual Pass holders will need to pre-book their times for some venues during weekends, school and public holidays.

Problems buying tickets online? Phone 1800 751 060 or email **supportaus@accesso.com**.

# National Gallery of Victoria

Why you should go: For the thousands of artworks and artifacts from all over the world spanning millennia. It's a beautifully designed building for exhibiting art, blurring the line between art gallery and museum. The collection is so huge it spills over into the **Ian Potter Centre: NGV Australia** at Federation Square (page 93).

Address: 180 St Kilda Road, Melbourne 3006

Phone: 03 8620 2222

Website: **www.ngv.melbourne**

How to get there: Take any tram going down St Kilda Road. On a pleasant day it's also just a 15-minute amble from Flinders Street.

Opening hours: 10.00 am to 5.00 pm seven days.

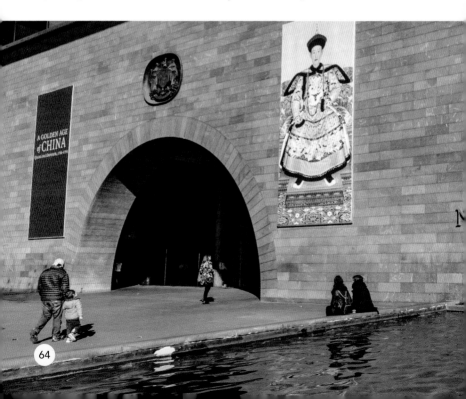

Time budget: At least three hours to do the place justice.

For the virtual visitor: To enhance your visitor experience, the NGV has an app that you can download from the website.

How much? FREE but donations are always welcome. Special exhibitions incur additional charges but are worth the expense as many of them are once-in-a-lifetime opportunities to see particular works of art and collections.

While you're here: The **Arts Centre Melbourne** (page 91) is right next door. **Southbank** (page 126) is a short walk north-west and the **Royal Botanic Gardens** (page 57) are a short walk south-east. A 10-minute walk south-west along Sturt Street will take you to the **Australian Centre for Contemporary Art** (page 92).

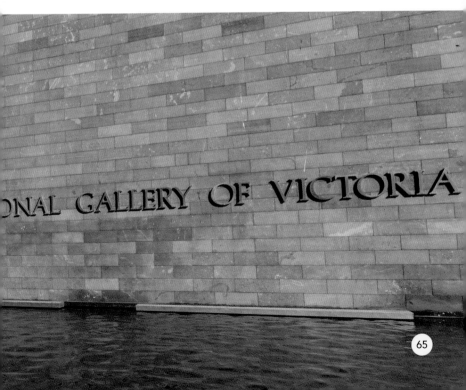

# Museums and Other Cultural Institutions

Melbourne has some of the best museums in Australia and space limitations allow us only to mention a few of the most popular. However, if you're a total museum buff then explore the listings at Australian Museums and Galleries: **www.aumuseums.com**.

## Melbourne Cricket Ground and the National Sports Museum

Why you should go: Cricket is arguably a religion in Australia, and AFL football is almost certainly a religion in Victoria, and both are played with alarming frequency at the national shrine that is the Melbourne Cricket Ground – and almost everybody calls it the **MCG**. This is the tenth largest stadium in the world, the largest in the Southern Hemisphere, the largest cricket ground by capacity – 100,024 seats to be exact – and it has really tall lights. It also hosts the occasional rock concert and other public events.

The **National Sports Museum**, is also located on the grounds of the MCG and includes the **Australian Racing Museum**, **Cricket Club Museum** and the **Australian Sports Hall of Fame**.

Please note that at the time of writing the **National Sports Museum** was closed for refurbishment and due to reopen in early 2020.

Address: Brunton Avenue, Richmond 3002

Phone: MCG – 03 9657 8888; NSM – 03 9657 8879

Websites: **www.mcg.org.au**; **www.nsm.org.au**

How to get there: Take the train to Jolimont Station and walk south for two minutes through Jolimont Reserve and Yarra Park or alternatively go to Richmond Station and walk north-west across Yarra Park for five minutes.

Opening hours: For the museum, 10.00 am to 5.00 pm seven days except for modified hours on MCG event days.

Time budget: At least two hours.

How much? Tickets are available for National Sports Museum entry only, MCG tour only, or for both. Since you've come this far, you might as well do both as a package and save money. The tour alone takes 75 minutes because the MCG is big, and they run between 10.00 am and 3.00 pm daily; adults $35, concessions $29, children $18 and families (2 adults, 2 children) $76, $5 for additional children over 5, children under 5 FREE. For non-package tickets go to: **www.nsm.org.au/visit/tickets**.

While you're here: You're not far from shops of Bridge Road in Richmond, and the cafes and pubs of Swan and Church streets. The more energetic can easily walk back to the CBD using the William Barak Bridge. It's just over 1 kilometer (½ mile) to walk and should take you about 10 to 15 minutes.

# Melbourne Observatory

Why you should go: If you're a fan of the cosmos and all things celestial then naturally the Melbourne Observatory is worth a visit. Constructed between 1861 and 1863 much of the original equipment is still in use for studying the heavens.

Address: On the grounds of the **Royal Botanic Gardens** (page 57)

Phone: 03 9252 2300

Website: **www.rbg.vic.gov.au**

How to get there: Take any of the trams that go down St Kilda Road, or simply walk. It's a 15-minute, very pleasant walk from Flinders Street until you reach the northern perimeter of the gardens. **Alexandra Gardens** and **Queen Victoria Gardens** are at this northern perimeter. While they are not officially part of the Botanic Gardens, they are essentially an extension of this green area, and you can stroll through them on your way there.

Opening hours: Admission is generally by tour only. The **Starry Southern Skies** tours are run by volunteers from the Astronomical Society of Victoria and the gathering point is the **Melbourne Gardens Visitor Centre**.

Time budget: At least two hours.

How much? Adults $24, concessions and children (8–17) $20, families (4 individuals in any combination but should include at least one adult) $70. The website warns that the tours aren't suitable for children under 8 years old.

Also note: 'This tour includes entry into confined spaces and climbing stairs, therefore requires a moderate level of physical fitness and mobility. This is an indoor and outdoor activity. Please wear appropriate clothing for weather conditions and appropriate footwear.' Starting time is usually around 8.00 pm in winter, later in summer. The tour takes 90 minutes and bookings are made through the website.

While you're here: Since the tours run only at night, you'll want to do this at the end of the day after you've made merry elsewhere. Make sure you plan your day so that you have enough energy at the end of your day to enjoy the tour.

## Old Melbourne Gaol

Why you should go: Australia started off as one huge gaol (jail) for European settlers and no one can deny the enduring fascination of true-crime stories. Old Melbourne Gaol is Victoria's oldest surviving prison and describes itself as 'Melbourne's most haunting and spell-binding venue' – we think they mean this literally. Definitely one of those 'if these walls could speak' places, and here, they do.

Address: 377 Russell Street, between Victoria and La Trobe streets, Melbourne,3000

Phone: 03 9656 9889

Website: **www.oldmelbournegaol.com.au**

How to get there: Take the FREE tram 35 to the corner of La Trobe Street and Exhibition Street. Walk south-west along La Trobe until you get to Russell Street, then walk north for a couple of minutes.

Opening hours: 9.30 am to 5.00 pm seven days.

Time budget: At least an hour.

How much? Adults $28, concessions $23, children (5–15) $15, family (2 adults, 2 children) $65, family (1 adult, 2 children) $48, $5 per extra child. During school holidays check out the **Escape the Gaol** experience at no extra charge.

While you're here: The gaol has a number of special, after-hours tours on offer. Bookings essential so phone first to confirm times and make bookings or book online. Tours include the **Hangman's Night Tour, Ghosts? What Ghosts?** and **A Night in the Watch House.**

The **State Library of Victoria** (page 78) is a short walk to the south, walk further south and you'll reach **Chinatown** (page 125). **Melbourne Central** (page 126) is a slightly longer walk to the south-west.

## Parliament House

Why you should go: While politics isn't usually high on the traveler or tourist's list, Australia likes, at least in principle, to have open government, and visiting Parliament House when Parliament is in session is your chance to see democracy in action. The House offers a host of fascinating tours on a variety of different specialist subjects including architecture, art and gardening and they allow you access to areas that the public usually doesn't get to see. The best part is that both access to Parliament and the tours are FREE.

Address: 377 Russell Street (between Victoria and La Trobe streets), Melbourne 3000

Phone: 03 9651 8911

Website: **www.parliament.vic.gov.au**

How to get there: Take the train from Flinders Street Station to Parliament Station, then it's a short walk.

Opening hours: 8.30 am to 5.30 pm Monday to Friday.

Time budget: 1 to 1½ hours, longer if you're having high tea (see below).

How much? FREE! Australians pay for it all through their taxes.

While you're here: There are so many tours that are available at different times and on different days that we recommend that you just show up and see what's on offer. Most tours don't require bookings. However, if you like to plan ahead it's best to visit the website (**www.parliament.vic.gov.au/visit/public-tours**) or call the special tours line on 03 9651 8568 to check out tour times and durations. Please note that tours are subject to availability and can be cancelled if there's a function or other event on. For the virtual visitor there are also virtual tours: **www.parliament.vic.gov.au/visit/virtual-tour**. Parliament has also been serving high tea since 1924 on non-parliament sitting days, Monday to Friday between 2.30 pm and 4.00 pm. Cost: $50 per person.

Bourke Street is right in front of Parliament and you're a ten-minute stroll to **Bourke Street Mall** (page 124). The **Old Treasury Building and Gardens** (below) is a short walk along Spring Street to the south.

## Old Treasury Building and Treasury Gardens

Why you should go: This lovely piece of sandstone architecture, built at the height of the gold rush, manages to be both imposing and charming at the same time. It's dedicated to the history of Melbourne and Victoria and its people, but its viewpoint focuses on intimate storytelling. There are permanent exhibitions, including the gold vaults where gold was stored during the gold rush and important public records, as well as long-term and special exhibitions.

Address: 20 Spring Street Melbourne 3000

Phone: 03 9651 2233

Website: **www.oldtreasurybuilding.org.au**

How to get there: Take the train from Flinders Street Station to Parliament Station, then it's a short walk south.

Opening hours: 10.00 am to 4.00 pm Sunday to Friday.

Time budget: 1 to 1½ hours.

How much? FREE!

While you're here: Just north there's **Parliament House** (page 74). Just south there's the **Treasury Gardens**, a lovely place to have a picnic when the weather's up for it. Just east there's the **Fitzroy Gardens** (page 50). The whole of the CBD lies to the west so take your pick of where you want to go.

# Australian Centre for the Moving Image

Why you should go: It's a museum dedicated to the moving image – film, video and of course electronic media – with interactive exhibits, screen industry labs and virtual experiences. Note that at the time of writing ACMI was closed for renovations and due to reopen in mid-2020, but visit the website for offsite screenings.

Address: Federation Square, Melbourne 3000

Phone: 03 8663 220

Website: **www.acmi.net.au**

How to get there: It's a two-minute walk east from Flinders Street Station, on Flinders Street.

Opening hours: 10.00 am to 5.00 pm seven days.

Time budget: At least an hour.

How much? FREE but donations are always welcome. Special exhibitions incur additional charges.

While you're here: You're right in the heart of **Federation Square** (page 48) and centrally located in the CBD, so Melbourne is your oyster.

## State Library of Victoria

Why you should go: Because bibliophiles need few excuses to visit a library comprising 23 neoclassical buildings, one of which has a most amazing central, octagonal reading room.

Address: 328 Swanston Street, Melbourne 3000

Phone: 03 8664 7000

Website: **www.slv.vic.gov.au**

How to get there: Take the train from Flinders Street Station to Melbourne Central Station, get out at the La Trobe Street exit and it's across the road in Swanston Street.

Opening hours: 10.00 am to 9.00 pm Monday to Thursday, 10.00 am to 6.00 pm Friday to Sunday.

Time budget: 1 to 1½ hours, longer if you get engrossed in an exhibition or in a rare book on a rainy day.

How much? FREE!

While you're here: There are exhibitions, talks and lectures and events going on all the time, so phone or visit the website to see what's on. Take the FREE, half-hour-long Welcome Library Tour, departing every day from Readings Bookshop in the **Russell Street Welcome Zone** at 10.45 am. Also ask about other specialist tours that highlight special exhibitions. For further information call 03 8664 7099.

You're right in the middle of the CBD, but the nearest attraction is **Chinatown** (page 125), and you're not far from **Bourke Street Mall** (page 124), **Melbourne Central** (page 126) and **Old Melbourne Gaol** (page 72).

# The Multicultural Museums of Melbourne

Melbourne, along with London, New York and Sydney is one of the most cosmopolitan, diverse, multicultural cities in the English-speaking world, and as the cultural capital of Australia (Shhh! Don't let Sydney hear you say that!) it has a number of excellent museums showcasing not only Melbourne's, but Australia's rich cultural heritage.

Don't forget to visit the **Bunjilaka Aboriginal Cultural Centre** in the Melbourne Museum (page 51) while you're there too (**www.museumsvictoria.com.au/bunjilaka**).

# Chinese Museum

Why you should go: The story of the Chinese in Australia is over 200 years old but really kicks in with the Victorian gold rush of 1851, and Chinese immigrants have made huge contributions to Australia. There are three permanent exhibitions: **Chinese Australian History**, the **Dragon Gallery** and **Finding Gold**. Temporary exhibitions rotate around every three months.

Address: 22 Cohen Place, Melbourne 3000 (right in the heart of Chinatown)

Phone: 03 9662 2888

Website: **www.chinesemuseum.com.au**

How to get there: Take the FREE tram 35 to the corner of Lonsdale Street and Nicholson Street, or take the train to Parliament Street and get to the same place, then walk south-west down Lonsdale Street, past Exhibition Street, and the next lane on your left is Cohen Place.

Opening hours: 10.00 am to 4.00 pm seven days.

Time budget: About 1 to 1½ hours.

How much? Adults $11, concessions $9, families $26 (2 adults, 3 children). Special exhibits are all included in the entry fee.

While you're here: You're right in the heart of **Chinatown** (page 125), so there's plenty to see.

# Co.As.It Historical Society & Museo Italiano

Why you should go: After the Greeks, the Italians are the most significant European ethnicity represented in Melbourne. The Museo Italiano is curated by the Italian Historical Society which is in turn run by the Italian Assistance Association – Co.As.It.

Address: 199 Faraday Street, Carlton 3053

Phone: 03 9347 3555

Website: **www.coasit.com.au/museoitaliano**

How to get there: Take tram 16 from the Swanston Street/St Kilda Road entrance of Flinders Street Station to the corner of Faraday Street and Swanston Street, Carlton then walk east along Faraday Street for about 3 minutes.

Opening hours: 9.00 am to 5.00 pm Tuesday to Friday, noon to 5.00 pm Saturday.

Time budget: About 1 to 1½ hours.

How much? FREE for general admission. Community and cultural events might incur additional charges, but most are free.

While you're here: You're in the heart of Melbourne's Little Italy, so there are plenty of good places to eat nearby, with special mention to **Brunetti** (page 141).

Although nothing to do with Italian culture you're also a short walk from the **Ian Potter Museum of Art** (page 93) and the **Tracy Maund Historical Collection** with 5000 items relating to the Royal Women's Hospital. Admission to the Maund Collection is FREE but by appointment only; Address: 132 Grattan Street, Carlton 3053; Phone: 03 9344 2032; Website: **www.cv.vic.gov.au/ organisations/tracy-maund-historical-collection**.

In the opposite direction (south-east) you're only a 10-minute walk to **Melbourne Museum** and the **Royal Exhibition Building** (page 51).

# Hellenic Museum

Why you should go: Melbourne has the largest Greek community outside of Europe and you'd be hard-pressed to find a Melbournian who didn't have a friend or relative of Greek descent. Greek culture is arguably the cradle of Western civilization anyway, so you might as well find out what the Greeks have been doing both before and since they left the cradle. With a history spanning 8000 years there's plenty to see.

Address: 280 William Street, Melbourne 3000 (just near the corner of William Street and La Trobe Street)

Phone: 03 8615 9016

Website: **www.hellenic.org.au**

How to get there: Take the FREE tram 35 to the corner of La Trobe Street and William Street. From there it's just a short stroll south.

Opening hours: 10.00 am to 4.00 pm seven days.

Time budget: About two hours.

How much? Adults $10, concessions $5, children 6 years and under FREE! Special exhibits are all included in the entry fee.

While you're here: Kids might want to join the Argonauts Club: **www.argonautsclub.org/home**. Self-guided tours are also available: **www.hellenic.org.au/tours**. If your hankering for things Hellenic persists, you might consider lunch at the nearby **Grounds of Arcadia restaurant,** serving lunch from 11.30 am to 4.00 pm Tuesday to Friday.

A five-minute walk north-east up either La Trobe Street or Little Lonsdale Street will take you to **Melbourne Central** (page 126). A 10-minute walk south-east down William Street will take you to the **Immigration Museum** (page 85) and from there it's not far to **SEA LIFE Melbourne Aquarium** (page 106).

# Immigration Museum

Why you should go: Because apart from the Indigenous inhabitants, it could be argued that everyone else living in Australia is an immigrant. More to the point, almost 30 per cent of the current estimated resident population of Melbourne was born overseas. Almost half of all Australians were either born overseas or have at least one parent who was born overseas. You cannot possibly understand Australia unless you understand immigration and here's an institution dedicated to just that.

Address: 400 Flinders Street, Melbourne 3000

Phone: 131 102

Website: **www.museumsvictoria.com.au/immigrationmuseum**

How to get there: It's a five-minute walk west from Flinders Street Station.

Opening hours: 10.00 am to 5.00 pm seven days.

Time budget: At least an hour.

How much? Adults $15, everyone else, including concession card holders, FREE but donations are always welcome. Special exhibitions incur additional charges. You might also consider becoming a **Museums Victoria Member** (page 62) to get all sorts of additional benefits.

While you're here: You're centrally located in the CBD, so you can pretty much go anywhere, but the closest attraction is **SEA LIFE Melbourne Aquarium** (page 106). **Southbank** (page 126) and the **Eureka Skydeck** (page 46) are also very close and easily accessible via Queens Bridge, which is just opposite the museum.

## Islamic Museum of Australia

Why you should go: The Muslim community in Australia is substantial and significant and if you're one of those people who find the history of Islam fascinating then the Islamic Museum, with its five galleries and year-long program of special exhibitions and workshops, is one of the lesser-known gems of Melbourne. But you'll need to go just a little out of your way to get there.

Address: 15A Anderson Road, Thornbury 3071

Phone: 1300 915 171

Website: **www.islamicmuseum.org.au**

How to get there: At Flinders Street Station take tram 1 to East Coburg and get off at the corner of Holmes Street/Nicholson Street and Moreland Road, Brunswick (33 minutes). Walk east along Moreland road until you get to Anderson Road, turn left (north) and keep walking. The museum is on the west (left) side of the road (10 minutes). The whole trip should take you about 45 minutes.

Opening hours: 10.00 am to 4.00 pm Monday to Saturday, cafe open 9.00 am to 3.00 pm.

Time budget: About two hours.

How much? Adults $12, concessions $10, children (6 to 12 years) $8, families (2 adults, 2 children 12 and under) $35, children under 5 and teachers with ID FREE. Special exhibits are all included in the entry fee.

While you're here: For the virtual visitor, the Islamic Museum has an app: **www.islamicmuseum.org.au/tours**.

If you go back to where you got off the tram you'll be another five-minute walk from the corner of Moreland Road and Sydney Road. Here, you're at the upper central end of the suburb of **Brunswick**, known for its laid-back, counter-cultural, alternative-crowd feel. It's an off the beaten tourist track sort of experience to walk south down Sydney Road, and if you're still hankering for more of the Middle East there are plenty of eateries and specialty shops to choose from. Otherwise, it's back to the CBD for further adventures.

# Jewish Museum of Australia

Why you should go: This is a highly interactive museum where you can learn a lot about various aspects of Jewish culture with the museum's five permanent exhibitions. Special programs often involve food – both the cooking and the eating.

Address: 26 Alma Road, St Kilda 3182

Phone: 03 8534 3600

Website: **www.jewishmuseum.com.au**

How to get there: Take tram 3 or 3a to St Kilda to the corner of Alma Road and the Nepean Highway. Walk north up the highway and turn left (east) into Alma Road and walk for less than a minute. The museum is on the left.

Opening hours: 10.00 am to 4.00 pm Tuesday, Wednesday, Thursday, 10.00 am to 3.00 pm Friday, 10.00 am to 5.00 pm Sunday, closed Saturday and Monday, public holidays and Jewish Holy Days.

Time budget: About 1 to 1½ hours.

How much? Adults $12, concessions and children (6 to 17 years) $6, family (2 adults, 2 children or 1 adult, 3 children) $27, children under 5 FREE. Special exhibits and programs might incur additional charges.

While you're here: You're right in the heart of **St Kilda** (page 127), so there's plenty to see, including **Luna Park** (page 110).

If you're particularly interested in the Jewish Holocaust then also consider a visit to the **Jewish Holocaust Centre** at 13–15 Selwyn Street, Elsternwick 3185; Phone: 03 9528 1985; Website: **www.jhc.org.au**. Open every day except Saturday. Just catch a train from Flinders Street Station to Elsternwick Station then it's a short walk east down Glen Huntly Road until you reach Selwyn Street.

# Arty Stuff

Melbourne is so rich in art galleries and other artistically oriented attractions that the visitor is spoiled for choice. An art guide to Melbourne would be a substantial book just in and of itself.

Here then is a list of just some of the more prominent highlights of Melbourne's fine arts and performing arts scene. It's an eclectic list, so there's likely to be at least a few places that will satisfy every artistic taste. Many of these venues are mainstream but some are more boutiquey and might vary in their opening hours and what's on, so phone ahead or visit the websites for further information.

# Abbotsford Convent

Abbotsford Convent is about 4 kilometers (2.5 miles) from the CBD and this sprawling arts precinct on the site of a former convent (as the name suggests) is home to more than 100 studios, two galleries, cafes and gardens. Be sure to check out the **Convent Bakery** with its wood-fired breads too. The **Collingwood Childrens' Farm** is also on the grounds.

Address: 1 St Heliers Street, Abbotsford 3067
Phone: 03 9415 3600
Website: **www.abbotsfordconvent.com.au**

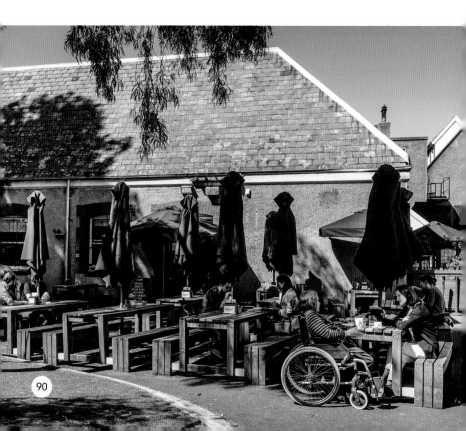

# Arts Centre Melbourne

This hard-to-miss iconic performing arts complex with its white central spire is right next to the **State Theatre** and the **National Gallery of Victoria** (page 64). All sorts of stuff goes on here including classical music, ballet and theater. Guided tours are available (11 am Monday to Saturday; adults $25, children $15) and backstage tours run every Sunday at 11 am and cost $30. Self-guided tours are also available.

Address: 100 St Kilda Road, Melbourne 3004

Phone: 1300 182 183

Website: **www.artscentremelbourne.com.au**

# Australian Centre for Contemporary Art

It's just what it says it is and, as a bonus, is housed in a striking rusted steel building. It's just a short walk down Sturt Street from the **National Gallery of Victoria** (page 64) or catch tram 1 from St Kilda Road.

Address: 111 Sturt Street, Southbank 3006
Phone: 03 9697 9999
Website: **www.acca.melbourne**

# Centre for Contemporary Photography

Features five exhibition spaces for contemporary photography by local, interstate and international artists.

Address: 404 George Street, Fitzroy 3065
Phone: 03 9417 1549
Website: **www.cpp.org.au**

# Gertrude Contemporary

A venue that is both a contemporary arts space and working artists' studios.

Address: 21–31 High Street, Preston 3072
Phone: 03 9419 3406
Website: **www.gertrude.org.au**

## Ian Potter Centre: NGV Australia

This is the part of the National Gallery of Victoria that specializes in Australian art from historic Indigenous art to contemporary pieces and artifacts, including photography, fashion and decorative arts. The Ian Potter Centre also hosts special exhibitions. Located conveniently in the heart of **Federation Square** (page 48).
Address: Federation Square, Melbourne 3000
Phone: 03 8620 2222
Website: **www.ngv.vic.gov.au**

## Ian Potter Museum of Art

Founded in 1972 as the University of Melbourne's art museum, this is a very eclectic art museum and exhibition space that, aside from its permanent collection of art spanning thousands of years, seems to have no focus rather than whatever happens to be interesting at the time, and it doesn't disappoint. Note that at the time of writing the museum was undergoing redevelopment so be sure to check the website for the current opening hours before visiting.
Address: University of Melbourne, Swanston Street, Parkville 3010
Phone: 03 8344 5148
Website: **www.art-museum.unimelb.edu.au**

## Heide Museum of Modern Art

Located about 20 minutes from the CBD on the site of a former dairy farm that was once the home of Melbourne arts benefactors John and Sunday Reed. 'Heide', as it is affectionately known, was named after the Heidelberg art movement and was sold to the Victorian Government for an art museum and park in 1980. A unique combination of art, sculpture, architecture, social history and landscape, Heide's collection includes works by significant Australian artists such as Sidney Nolan, John Perceval, Joy Hester and Arthur Boyd. Spot kangaroos in the nearby parks too!

Address: 7 Templestowe Road, Bulleen 3105

Phone: 03 9850 1500

Website: **www.heide.com.au**

## Lyon Housemuseum

Located at 219 Cotham Road, Kew 3101 is another one of Melbourne's better kept secrets. The Lyon Housemuseum is a unique combination of family residence and private museum and displays the Lyon Collection of contemporary Australian art. The Housemuseum is open for pre-booked tours on designated days. Being a private home there are a number of rules for visitors, including no children under 12 allowed (**www.lyonhousemuseum.com.au/visit/tours**). It's a little out of the way but if you're interested in unusual approaches to museums it's a must see.

The **Housemuseum Galleries**, just next door at 217 Cotham Road, is open to the public from Tuesdays to Sundays from 10.00 am to 5.00 pm. Visit **www.lyonhousemuseum.com.au** for more details of what's on.

The properties are easily accessible on tram 109 to Box Hill. Get on at Collins Street in the CBD and get off at Florence Avenue. The trip takes about 40 minutes but can take up to an hour in peak traffic times.

## District Docklands Makers Market

Not only art but design, craft, jewelry and food in the District Docklands shopping center main atrium on Docklands Drive. It's easily reached on the FREE tram 35. Open on the last Sunday of every month and it's totally enclosed, so you don't have to worry about the weather.

Website: **www.rosestmarket.com.au/docklandsmarket**

## Rose Street Artists Market

Located in hip Fitzroy, this is your opportunity to actually buy or even commission art from local artists. Up to 120 creative artists showcase everything from furniture to fashion and jewelry, ceramics and artworks each weekend. To get there catch tram 96 from Bourke Street or tram 11 from Collins Street.

Address: 60 Rose Street, Fitzroy 3065 (between Brunswick and Nicholson streets)

Opening hours: Open 10.00 am to 4.00 pm every weekend.

Website: **www.rosestmarket.com.au**

## Melbourne Street Art Tours

For those who like street art (formally known as high-end graffiti) these tours hire practicing Melbourne street artists as their guides. There are CBD and Fitzroy tours on offer. CBD tours end at Blender Studios with a tour of the studios and gallery. Tours last approximately three hours and cost from $69 for adults and $35 for children.

Address: Blender Studios, 33–35 Dudley Street, West Melbourne 3003

Phone: 03 9328 5556; 0416 971 708

Website: **www.melbournestreettours.com**

## Urban Scrawl Tours

Run by art historians, tours include the Melbourne City Laneway Arts Tour and a Fitzroy and Collingwood Street Art Tour. Tour times are flexible and by appointment only. Adults $35, concessions $30.

Phone: 0434 167 647

Website: **www.urbanscrawl.com.au/tours**

# Fun with the Kids

Some attractions are more child-friendly while others are specifically designed to appeal to the under 18s, especially if your kids are really young. Here are some places to visit that you can bring the whole family to that have gone that extra mile to keep the kiddies entertained.

# Chesterfield Farm and the Melbourne Steam Traction Engine Club at the National Steam Centre

Why you should go: Chesterfield Farm is an excellent way to introduce kids to the realities of farm life. The National Steam Centre is a must for steam enthusiasts.

Address: 1221 Ferntree Gully Road, Scoresby 3179

Phone: 03 9763 1588

Website: **www.chesterfieldfarm.com.au**

How to get there: Both these attractions are close to each other, but a little out of the way. If you don't have a car and you're prepared for an hour and 15-minute journey each way then catch the train to Glen Waverly Station and connect with bus 753 that will take you almost to the doorstep of the farm.

Opening hours: 10.00 am to 3.00 pm Monday to Friday, 10.00 am to 5.00 pm Saturday and Sunday.

Time budget: Realistically it's an all-day trip including travel time, particularly if you're visiting both venues.

How much? Adults $15, concessions $13, children (6 to 17 years) $9, family (2 adults, 2 children or 1 adult, 3 children) $40, $3 per person for tractor rides, children under 3 FREE.

While you're here: If visiting Chesterfield on the weekend (from 11.00 am to 4.00 pm and occasionally on Thursdays), you're right across the road from a collection of over 800 exhibits housed in the National Steam Centre. If it's connected with a steam engine, you'll find it here. The NSC is entirely run by volunteers and donations and charges no entry fee, so feel free to be generous with a donation. For more details phone 03 9763 1614 or visit the website: **www.melbournesteam.com.au**.

# The Theme of Steam

Melbourne just loves its steam engines …

## Diamond Valley Miniature Railway

Address: Eltham Lower Park, 570 Main Road, Eltham 3095
Phone: 03 9439 1493
Website: **www.dvr.com.au**
How to get there: Catch a train to Eltham Railway Station, then bus 513 to The Park.
When: Runs every Sunday from 11.00 am to 5.00 pm.
Time budget: About an hour.
How much? $3 per person per ride, children under 2 ride FREE.
While you're here: If you're going to go this far out, you might as well continue on and visit **Montsalvat** (page 117). On Main Road catch bus 902 to Airport West SC and stop at Mount Pleasant Road. From there catch bus 582 to Eltham Station to Hillcrest Avenue. Be warned, if you're on public transport be prepared for a slightly challenging uphill walk up Hillcrest Avenue.

## Puffing Billy

Puffing Billy is arguably the most famous steam locomotive in Australia, passing through the stunning rainforest scenery of the Dandenong Ranges, 40 kilometers (25 miles) east of Melbourne.
Address: 1 Old Monbulk Road, Belgrave 3160
Phone: 03 9757 0700
Website: **www.puffingbilly.com.au**
How to get there: Catch a train to Belgrave Railway Station. It's a one-hour trip from Flinders Street but Puffing Billy is worth it.

When: Runs every day from 9.00 am to 5.00 pm.

Time budget: Puffing Billy stops at Emerald and then goes on to Lakeside (one hour) or all the way to Gembrook (two hours) and stops for a rest and recuperation for about two hours at Gembrook. By the time you've factored in the return trip from Flinders Street, we're talking an all-day commitment here. You won't have the time or energy to do anything else.

How much? Prices vary seasonally, but to give you a rough idea a Belgrave to Gembrook open return ticket for a family (2 adults and up to 4 children) is $155. Weekday discounts are sometimes available so phone or check on the website. Bookings for all journeys and experiences essential.

While you're here: If you really want the total experience, then try these options: **Steam and Cuisine** – trip and three-course lunch, adults $115, concessions and children (5 to 16

years) $105; **Steam and Cuisine After Dark** – trip and three-course dinner, $115 per person; **Murder on the Puffing Billy Express** – trip, three-course dinner and live show, a four-and-a-half-hour extravaganza trip every Saturday 7.00 pm to 11:30 pm, $120 per person, usually booked out two months in advance, so think ahead! Dress in a 1920s theme to really join in the fun.

## Steamrail Victoria

Steamrail Victoria is a volunteer organization dedicated to the preservation of vintage locomotives. Throughout the year they have special excursions and tours where you have the opportunity to experience some heavy-duty steam train action. Tours can range from short suburban rides to major rides to regional centers. Tickets range from as little as $20 for adults, $10 for children and $50 for families for short trips to over $500 per head for major weekend tours that include sleeping cars, overnight stays, dinners and side trips to wineries. This one is for *serious* rail enthusiasts.

Phone: 03 9397 1953

Website: **www.steamrail.com.au**

## Healesville Sanctuary

Located in the Yarra Valley, about an hour from Melbourne, this family-friendly zoo is perfect for exploring Australian native animals in a wildlife setting.

Address: Badger Creek Road, Badger Creek 3777

Phone: 1300 966 784

Website: **www.zoo.org.au/healesville**

How to get there: Catch a train to Lilydale Railway Station, then bus 685 to Healesville then bus 686 from Healesville to Healesville Sanctuary. Another option is to take the ZOObus direct shuttle from the city to Healesville Sanctuary. The shuttle station is located at the Russell Street Extension, off Flinders Street, behind Federation Square.

Opening hours: 9.00 am to 5.00 pm seven days.

Time budget: This is an all-day commitment, but the staff know that people come from far for a visit, so they go that extra mile to make each visit special.

How much? Adults (over 16 years) $37, seniors $33, concessions $28, children $19 Monday to Friday outside of holidays, FREE for children (4 to 15 years) on weekends, public holidays and during public school holidays. You might want to consider becoming a member (page 62), especially if you also plan to visit **Melbourne Zoo** (page 53) and **Werribee Open Range Zoo** (page 108).

While you're here: There are too many highlights to mention but the keeper talks about their special animals are of particular note. The fast-paced **Spirits of the Sky Bird Show**, **Tales from Platypus Creek**, **Animals of the Night** – the list just goes on and on …

## Punting on the Lake

Taking a punt out on the lake is a genteel and relaxed opportunity to experience the **Royal Botanic Gardens** in a unique way. The wooden punts are based on designs used in Cambridge, England, and with the punters also dressed traditionally in waistcoats and boater hats you could imagine yourself drifting down an English river. Punting is available only during the summer (except for high tea, see below) because fewer people want to go punting in the cold; although, if the weather's good, why not? Note: Only children under 12 are required to wear a (provided) life jacket, but they are available if they make you feel more comfortable.

Address: Ornamental Lake, Royal Botanic Gardens,
   South Yarra 3141

Phone: 0481 455 410

Website: **www.puntingonthelake.com.au**

How to get there: It's on the grounds of the **Royal Botanic Gardens** (page 57), so it's an easy stroll south down St Kilda Road.

Opening hours: 10.30 am to 5.00 pm seven days from September to May.

Time budget: About half an hour. Allow 2½ hours if you're doing high tea.

How much? Adults $25 (over 16 years), children $12, family (2 adults, up to 3 children) $65, well-behaved dogs (on a lead) FREE! Bookings essential.

While you're here: **Punting Boat Tour and High Tea** available September to May but also on weekends June to August (weather permitting, excluding public holidays). Book through the **Terrace Café**; Phone: 03 9820 9590; adults (over 16 years) $75, children (5 to 12) $55, infants (up to 4) FREE! You can bring your own picnic, or you can also order picnic boxes from the Terrace Café.

# SEA LIFE Melbourne Aquarium

This interactive, multilevel aquarium is home to more than 10,000 animals. There are saltwater crocodiles! There are sharks!

Address: Corner of King Street and Flinders Street, Melbourne 3000

Website: **www.melbourneaquarium.com.au** (all bookings and information online)

How to get there: It's a super-easy walk west along Flinders Street, or if you want, just catch FREE tram 35 to the corner of King Street and Flinders Street.

Opening hours: 10.00 am to 5.00 pm Monday to Friday, 9.30 am to 6.00 pm Saturday and Sunday.

Time budget: About two hours.

How much? Booking online prices: adults (over 16 years) $33.60, children $22.40. You might also consider saving with a **Melbourne Big Ticket pass** (page 63) for entry to **SEA LIFE** and **Legoland Discovery Centre** (page 107).

While you're here: The **Behind the Scenes & Glass Bottom Boat Experience** costs $55.80 for adults and $43.20 for children. The **Penguin Passport** costs $149 per person (14 and over only) and the **Shark Dive Xtreme** experience where you get up close and personal with the sharks is $299 per person (14 and over only). There are also **SEA LIFE Nights** events for the grown-ups only.

# LEGOLAND Discovery Centre

This is your chance to play with the world's most famous plastic bricks. During peak times entry is limited to three hours and there's a limit to the number of patrons at any one time too. During off-peak times you can stay as long as you like. Best to book online to guarantee a place. Most of the time adults must be accompanied by a child (and vice versa) but there are also special adult nights for the young-at-heart, held every Thursday.

Address: Level 2/1341 Dandenong Rd, Chadstone 3148
   (in Chadstone Shopping Centre)

Phone: 1800 026 576

Website: **www.legolanddiscoverycentre.com.au**

How to get there: Chadstone Shopping Centre likes to make it as easy as possible for visitors, so they have a FREE shuttle bus that take you there from Federation Square from a dedicated stop on the corner of Flinders Street and Russel Street. Buses also depart from SEA LIFE Aquarium on the corner of Flinders and King streets. For further information and to book your trip go to: **www.chadstone.com.au/tourist-shuttle-bus**.

Opening hours: Check the website for Discovery Centre hours but the LEGO store is open 9.30 am to 5.30 pm Monday to Wednesday, 9.30 am to 9.00 pm Thursday to Saturday and 9.30 am to 7.00 pm Sunday.

How much? Tickets start at adults $32.50 and children (3 to 15 years) $27.50 but there are deals on all the time and you might consider buying a **Melbourne Big Ticket or Merlin Pass** (page 63) if they're available.

Time budget: At least two hours.

While you're here: There's plenty to see and do around **Chadstone Shopping Centre** (page 124).

## Werribee Open Range Zoo, Victoria State Rose Garden and Werribee Park and Mansion

Australia's open-range, open-plain zoos are as close as you'll get to Africa while still being in the country and Werribee has the virtue of being arguably the most accessible, being 30 minutes by car from Melbourne and just a relatively short bus ride from Werribee Railway Station. The Victoria State Rose Garden and Werribee Park and Mansion are nearby too, so there's something for every member of even a multi-generational family.

Address: K Road, Werribee South 3030

Phone: 1300 966 784

Website: **www.zoo.org.au/werribee**

How to get there: Catch a train to Werribee Railway Station, then bus 439 to Werribee South to the zoo. The full trip is about 1¼ hours each way. If you can't wait for a public bus call Squires Coaches and see if you can arrange a private shuttle. Phone: 03 9748 5094; Website: **www.werribeeparkshuttle.com.au**, or just catch a cab: Werribee Taxi 0478 723 430.

Opening hours: 9.00 am to 5.00 pm seven days.

Time budget: This is, at the very least, a half-day commitment.

How much? Adults (over 16 years) $37, seniors $33, concessions $28, children (4 to 15 years) $19 Monday to Friday outside of holidays, FREE for children on weekends, public holidays and during public school holidays. You might consider becoming a member (page 62), especially if you also plan to visit **Melbourne Zoo** (page 53) and **Healesville Sanctuary** (page 103).

While you're here: Autopia Tours offer a **Werribee Zoo Tour** that includes a visit to Victoria State Rose Garden and the historic Werribee Mansion and its formal gardens; Phone: 03 9393 1333; Website: **www.autopiatours.com.au**. Or you can just visit them yourself; they're next to each other and a 10-minute walk south of the zoo on Main Road.

   **Victoria State Rose Garden** Phone: 0450 659 993 or 0419 007 382; Website: **www.vicstaterosegarden.com.au**; Entry FREE!

   **Werribee Mansion** Website: **www.parkweb.vic.gov.au/explore/parks/werribee-park**.

# Luna Park Melbourne

This park on the shores of St Kilda with its 20-some rides is as close as you'll get to a traditional fairground in Melbourne. Luna Park is one of Melbourne's icons. Dating from 1912, visiting it is a total nostalgia trip.

Address: 18 Lower Esplanade, St Kilda 3182

Phone: 03 9525 5033

Website: **www.lunapark.com.au**

When: At least from 11.00 am to 6.00 pm Saturday and Sunday as well as school and public holidays. Hours extended during the warmer months.

How much? Entry only tickets are $5 if you just want to look around and not ride anything. Unlimited ride tickets are adults (13+) $49.95, children (4 to 12 years) $39.95, children (0 to 3 years) $17.50, family (2 adults, 2 children or 1 adult, 3 children) $149.95. Annual passes also available.

How to get there: Take tram 16 from Flinders Street Station to the last stop. The trip takes about 30 minutes.

Time budget: At least three hours.

While you're here: There's plenty to see and do around **St Kilda** (page 127).

## Melbourne Star Observation Wheel

This Ferris wheel on steroids is Melbourne's answer to the London Eye and offers panoramic views of the city's skyline. They call their rides 'flights' and the last flight departs 30 minutes prior to closing time.

Address: The District, Docklands 3008

Phone: 03 8688 9688

Website: **www.melbournestar.com**

Opening hours: At least 11.00 am to 7.00 pm seven days. Hours extended during the warmer months.

How much? Prices start from adults $36, concessions $28 and children (5 to 15 years) $22 but there are deals all the time. If you're visiting in the off-season you might even get a FREE child ticket for every adult one purchased. Bookings essential.

How to get there: Take the FREE tram 35 to Docklands. It's a five-minute walk north through **The District** shopping precinct.

Time budget: At least 30 minutes.

While you're here: There's plenty to see and do around the **Docklands** precinct (page 125).

## Scienceworks, The Lightning Room and Melbourne Planetarium

Scienceworks is Melbourne's family-oriented interactive science and technology museum and activity space. Permanent exhibits and a dynamic program of temporary exhibits constantly compete for your attention. The **Lightning Room** is a special exhibit that spectacularly showcases the properties of electrical weather. The Planetarium has special shows about the night sky.

Address: 2 Booker Street, Spotswood 3015

Phone: 03 8688 9688

Website: **www.museumsvictoria.com.au/scienceworks**

Opening hours: 10.00 am to 4.30 pm seven days.

How much? Adults (over 16 years) $15. If you have any other sort of concession that the museum accepts, entry is FREE, although surcharges apply for special exhibitions. You might consider becoming a Member (page 62), especially if you're also planning

to visit **Melbourne Museum** (page 51) and the **Immigration Museum** (page 85). The Lightning Room is an additional $8 per person per show. Melbourne Planetarium is an additional $8 per person per show. You might be able to save a little by buying an all-inclusive ticket. Just ask when you're purchasing.

How to get there: Take the train to Spotswood Station, then it's a short stroll north up Hall Street, turn right (east) at Hudson Road. Follow Hudson to its end then turn right (south) at Booker Street. The trip takes about 30 minutes.

Time budget: At least three hours, but you could easily spend the day here.

While you're here: Think about having lunch or dinner at the relatively close by **The Rose Hotel** (Phone: 03 9397 6259) or even **The Titanic Theatre Restaurant** (Phone: 03 9397 5101), or head back to the CBD – assuming you have any energy left after all the fun.

# Fun If You Have the Time

If you're staying longer in Melbourne, or if you've been before and want to experience things just ever-so-slightly off the beaten tourist path, here are a few things you might like to try.

## Melbourne River Cruises

Melbourne's largest river cruise operator offers sightseeing cruises across the city as well as through Docklands and to Williamstown. There is also a cruising restaurant.
Phone: 03 8610 2600
Website: **www.melbcruises.com.au**

## Yarra River Cruises

Offers a range of sightseeing cruises through the heart of the city.
Phone: 03 8488 8880
Website: **www.yarrarivercruises.com.au**

## Phillip Island Penguin Spotting

Phillip Island is 140 kilometers (87 miles) south of Melbourne. Each night at dusk the adorable little penguins return after a day fishing at sea and waddle up the beach to their burrows. Be warned that the penguins are very popular and busloads of tourists all try to get the best view. Your best option on a short visit will be to arrange a tour from Melbourne to Phillip Island. It is also possible to see little penguins at St Kilda pier without having to leave the city.
Phone: 03 95951 2800
Website: **www.visitphillipisland.com/listing/penguin-parade** or
　**www.penguins.org.au**

## Cheetham Wetlands

The Cheetham Wetlands are 420 hectares (about 1040 acres) on the western shores of Port Phillip Bay comprising both natural and artificial lagoons that preserve a natural saltmarsh ecology. This is one for the eco-tourist and the passionate bird watcher.

Website: **www.parkweb.vic.gov.au/explore/parks/ point-cook-coastal-park/tours**

How to get there: Take the train to Williams Landing Railway Station and then bus 497 to Point Cook Road and Saltwater Promenade. The trip takes about an hour.

## Cranbourne Botanic Gardens

The Cranbourne extension of the Royal Botanic Gardens is located about 45 kilometers (28 miles) south-east of the CBD and boasts a variety of wonders in its own right including the **Native Australian Garden**, with its stunning **Red Sand Garden**.

Address: Corner of Ballarto Road and Botanic Drive, Cranbourne 3977

Phone: 03 5990 2200

Website: **rbg.vic.gov.au/whats-on/list/all/Cranbourne**

Opening hours: 9.00 am to 5.00 pm seven days.

How to get there: Take the train to Cranbourne Railway Station and then bus 796 to the corner of South Gippsland Highway and Ballarto Road. The trip takes about 1½ hours.

## Montsalvat

Montsalvat is a unique artists colony in the north-eastern suburb of Eltham. Montsalvat is Australia's oldest continuously active artists' community with peaceful gardens, a restaurant, exhibitions, festivals, concerts, workshops and artists' residencies.

Address: 7 Hillcrest Avenue, Eltham 3095

Website: 03 9439 7712

Website: **www.montsalvat.com.au** or **montsalvat.com.au/whats-on**

Opening hours: 9.00 am to 5.00 pm seven days.

How to get there: Take the train to Eltham Railway Station and then bus 582 to the corner of Mount Pleasant Road and Rockliffe Street. The trip takes about 1½ hours. Be prepared for a bit of a climb up Rockliffe Street.

How much? Adults $14, concessions $10, children (5 to 12 years) $8, children under 5 FREE, families (2 adults and up to 3 children under 13) $35.

## Yarra Valley Winetasting Tours

The Yarra Valley has ideal growing conditions for various grape varieties and the wines of the region have a robust international reputation. A variety of operators offer tours of different wineries in the area. This is really one for the grown-ups, but the youngsters can take in the fresh country air and scenery.

Prices start from $99 per person to $250 for a more luxurious ride in a Mercedes Benz van including food as well as wine. You can even combine a wine tour with **Puffing Billy** (page 99).

## Be Part of a Television Audience

A lot of television production happens in Melbourne, especially comedy and variety shows that like to have a live studio audience. Attendance is FREE, but you'll need to book for this unique experience. Who knows, you might even end up as a contestant or part of a cast!

Website: **onlymelbourne.com.au/audience-required-tv-shows**

## Impossible Occurrences: Melbourne's Magic Show

Magician Luke Hocking performs a weekly show at the up-market Marriott Hotel. Guests are encouraged to dress up.

Address: Marriott Hotel, corner of Lonsdale and Exhibition streets, Melbourne 3000

Website: **www.impossibleoccurrences.com.au**

How much? $83 per person dinner and show package, $35 per person show only.

## Theater

Melbourne is Australia's theater capital with dozens of well-known theaters and shows premiering in the city. There's always something on to suit, whatever your tastes. Visit **www.onlymelbourne.com.au/theatre-show-melbourne** to see what's showing during your visit.

## Comedy

Melbourne has more comedy clubs than any other city in Australia. In the city that loves to laugh you can book a whole week of comedy nights. Comedy can be ephemeral, so the list below is just a rough guide and we recommend that you double-check what's going on with the venues before rocking up.

## Monday

Monday Comedy at Boney, 68 Little Collins Street, Melbourne
   3000; Phone: 03 9663 8268; Website: **www.boney.net.au**;
   6.30 pm to 8.30 pm; FREE entry, donations welcome.
Comedy at Spleen, 41 Bourke Street, Melbourne 3000
Phone: 03 9650 2400; Website: **www.comedyatspleen.com**;
   8.30 pm to 10.30 pm; FREE entry.

## Tuesday

Catfish Comedy, 30–32 Gertrude Street, Fitzroy 3065
Phone: 03 9417 6420; Website: **www.facebook.com/catfishcomedy**;
   8.00 pm to 10.00 pm; $12 entry.
Lido Comedy Tuesdays at the Jazz Room, Lido Cinemas,
   675 Glenferrie Road, Hawthorn 3122; Phone: 03 9818 7567;
   Website: **www.lidocinemas.com.au/events/lido-comedy**; 7.30 pm
   to 9.30 pm; FREE entry, donations welcome. FREE popcorn too!

## Six Days a Week including Wednesday

Live Comedy Show at the Comic's Lounge, 26 Errol Street,
   North Melbourne 3051; Phone: 03 9348 9488;
   Website: **www.thecomicslounge.com.au**; dinner at 7.00 pm,
   show at 8.00 pm to 10.30 pm Monday to Saturday; $20 for
   the show, more for the food.

## Thursday

Thursday Comedy Club at European Bier Café,
   120 Exhibition Street, Melbourne 3000;
   Phone: 0438 660 836 or 03 9663 1222;
   Website: **www.europeanbiercafe.com.au/event/
   thursday-night-comedy-club**; 8.30 pm to 11:00 pm; $12 entry.

## Friday

Comedy at the Coopers Inn, 282 Exhibition Street, Melbourne
3000; Phone: 03 9639 2111; Website: **www.coopersinn.com.au/
comedy**; 8.00 pm to 10.00 pm; $15 entry.

The Big HOO-HAA Improv Comedy Show at the Butterfly Club
at 5 Carson Place, Melbourne 3000; Phone: 03 9663 8107;
Website: **www.thebutterflyclub.com/show/the-big-hoo-haa**;
doors open 7:30 for an 8.00 pm to 10.00 pm show; adults $29,
concessions $25.

## Saturday

Basement Comedy Club at European Bier Café,
120 Exhibition Street, Melbourne 3000; Phone: 0438 660 836
or 03 9663 1222: Website: **www.europeanbiercafe.com.au/
event/basement-comedy-club-every-saturday-night**; 8.00 pm
to 10.00 pm; prices vary and you may need to buy tickets in
advance so check the website for details.

## Sunday

Club Voltaire Comedy Sundays, 14 Raglan Street,
North Melbourne 3051; Phone: 03 9326 3006;
Website: **www.facebook.com/clubvoltairecomedy**;
7.30 pm to 9.30 pm; gold coin donation depending on how
many laughs you get.

St Kilda Comedy Club Big Mouth Room, 168 Acland
Street, St Kilda 3182; Phone: 03 9534 4611;
Website: **www.stkildacomedyclub.com.au/
big-mouth-comedy-every-sunday-from-4pm**; 7.00 pm to 9.30 pm;
FREE entry, donations welcome.

# Streets and Streets of Shopping

# Clothing and Fashion

Melbourne is famous for its shopping – particularly for clothes and fashion. People have been known to fly to Melbourne with empty luggage and return with suitcases on the verge of bursting because you'll get stuff in Melbourne that you won't get anywhere else, and cheaper too!

## *Bridge Road*

Bridge Road cuts right through the suburb of Richmond, just to the east of the CBD, and you can pick up some truly amazing finds in the factory outlets. Bridge Road also has some great eateries and drinkeries, some of which you really have to seek out, but the fun is all in the search.

Website: **www.bridgerd.com.au**

## *Brunswick Street*

Confusingly, Brunswick Street isn't in the suburb of Brunswick but runs north–south in Fitzroy from Edinburgh Gardens in the north to Johnston Street in the south. It's one of Melbourne's more bohemian streets – eclectically funky and packed with interesting bars, pubs, cafes and shops.

Website: **www.www.brunswickstreet.com.au**

## *Gertrude Street*

Runs west to east in the southern quarter of Fitzroy, just north-east of the CBD. It's another of those eclectic streets but if you're looking for something unique to wear, this is where you'll find a lot of Melbourne's boutique labels.

## Chapel Street

Running north to south from the Yarra River to Balaclava south-east of the CBD, it's the bit that runs through South Yarra in the north and Prahran (pronounced 'Parran' with the 'Par' almost mumbled and the emphasis on 'ran') further south that is another of the hubs of high fashion. But there's so much else going on here too that it's easy to spend the day, and thousands of dollars if you like indulging your curiosity and your senses.

Website: **www.chapelstreet.com.au**

## Collins Street

In the heart of the CBD, parallel to Bourke Street to the north and Flinders Street to the south. Collins Street is an up-market shopping strip focused on high fashion and accessories, as well as plenty of great eating and drinking options. It has 70 cafes, bars and restaurants, 59 fashion outlets and 63 specialty shops. There's lots more because a whole bunch of lanes branch off Collins Street. Of special note is the **Block Arcade** near the corner of Collins Street and Elizabeth Street, a spectacular example of Victorian architecture with some, high-end boutique shopping.

Website: **www.theblock.com.au**

## Smith Street

Forms the east–west divide between Collingwood and Fitzroy, just to the north-east of the CBD. It's known for its factory outlets (at the northern end), but the varied southern end is where you'll find unusual providores and vintage clothing.

Website: **www.smithstreet.net.au**

### Sydney Road

A Melbourne exception in that it runs north for 24 kilometers (15 miles) without changing its name, but it is its southern end, where it runs right down the middle of Brunswick, which is arguably the most interesting bit for the traveler. This is where you really go for vintage and vintage-type clothing, as well as stores and co-ops run by independent designers. It's a street of constant change.

Website: **www.sydneyroad.com.au**

## The Arcades, Malls and Districts

### Bourke Street and Bourke Street Mall

Bourke Street runs south-west to north-east, right through the CBD, and **Bourke Street Mall**, that runs between Swanston Street and Elizabeth Street, is effectively the center of Melbourne. It has 84 cafes, bars and restaurants and 70 fashion outlets, and that's just for starters.

Website: **www.bourkestreet.com.au**

### Chadstone Shopping Centre

Arguably the biggest shopping mall in Australia. It's certainly the richest doing about $1.5 billion worth of business for its 20 million visitors a year. If size matters, and you want to mingle with the locals, go to Chadstone. There's even a FREE shuttle bus that will take you there and back from various locations in the city.

Website: **www.chadstone.com.au** and
**www.chadstone.com.au/tourist-shuttle-bus**

## Chinatown

Stepping through Chinatown's traditional huge red arches is like entering another world. Melbourne's Chinatown dates back to the goldrush of the 1850s and is the oldest continuous Chinese settlement in the Western world. It's centered around the eastern half of Little Bourke Street in the CBD.

Website: **www.chinatownmelbourne.com.au**

## Curtin House

Located at 252 Swanston Street in the CBD, it's worthy of a special mention because it looks like a Venetian Palazzo and has some amazing shops, eating and drinking options. The brilliantly designed website is worth visiting just for its own sake.

Website: **www.curtinhouse.com**

## Docklands

A sort of north-west extension of the Melbourne CBD, Docklands is an example of significant urban redevelopment. What was once a working, industrial dock is now a gentrified zone of specialty shops and things to amuse, easily reached with the FREE tram 35 and centered around **The District** shopping center. Docklands was the 2004 winner of The Australian Award for Urban Design.

Website: **www.thedistrictdocklands.com.au**

## Flinders Street

Home of Flinders Street Station, Flinders Street defines the southern border of the CBD. At the south-west end it meets up with Spencer Street and the spectacular **Spencer Street Railway Station**, one of those railway stations worth visiting just for its own sake. Further east along Flinders Street is the **SEA LIFE Melbourne Aquarium** (page 106) and further east still is the corner of Flinders Street and Swanston Street/St Kilda Road – the main entrance to Flinders Street Station and a major tram hub – as well as **Federation Square** (page 48).
Website: **www.flindersstreet.com.au**

## Melbourne Central

On the corner of La Trobe Street and Swanston Street is the CBD's biggest shopping mall, boasting almost 300 stores. It's dominated by a spectacular central atrium with a 20-story-high glass cone, specifically built to protect the National Trust registered **Coop's Shot Tower**. Other features include a **Marionette Watch** with a two-tonne chain and a soil-less **Vertical Garden**. It's easily reached by its own Melbourne Central Railway Station.
Website: **www.melbourncentral.com.au**

## Southbank and Southbank Promenade

Straddling the south bank of the Yarra River south of Flinders Street station, it's centered around the eclectic **Southgate Shopping Centre**.
Website: **www.southgatemelbourne.com.au**

For the truly adventurous, try two hours' worth of abseiling down one of Southbank's buildings with **Rap Jumping** at 334 City Road, Southbank; Phone: 1300 780 266; Website: **www.rapjumping.com.**

## St Kilda

St Kilda is a world all its own, a lively buffet of bohemian activity by the sea. Come for the atmosphere, but more than anything come here to *eat*. It has some of the best patisseries in Melbourne (page 141). There's also **Luna Park** (page 110), the **Jewish Museum** (page 88), and St Kilda is renowned for its pubs and live music. Easily reached by tram 16 from Swanston Street/St Kilda Road or, by a slightly more express route that takes you past **South Melbourne Markets** (page 60) on the light rail tram 96 that leaves from the corner of Flinders Street and Elizabeth Street on the north side of Flinders Street Station.

Website: **www.stkildamelbourne.com.au**.

# Once A Year If You Can Make It

Melbourne is renowned for its big public events and festivals and you might want to plan your trip around a particular interest.

# January

## *Australian Open Tennis at Melbourne Park*

One of the four tennis grand slams, attracting tennis fans from around the world during the last fortnight in January.
Website: **www.ausopen.com**

## *Midsumma Festival*

Melbourne's celebration of queer culture is held in mid-January each year and includes musicals, theater, cabaret, film and dance parties as well as the day-long celebration, Carnival.
Website: **www.midsumma.org.au**

# February

## *Chinese New Year*

Features several weeks of celebration and festivities and includes, food, firecrackers and the awakening of the dragon.
Website: **www.melbournechinesenewyear.com**

# March

## *Formula 1 Grand Prix*

The Australian Formula 1 Grand Prix is held at Albert Park and is usually the first event of the annual grand prix circuit.
Website: **www.grandprix.com.au**

### The Moomba Festival

Australia's largest FREE community festival happens on the Labour Day long weekend – one long family-friendly carnival along the banks of the Yarra in the CBD.

Website: **www.moomba.melbourne.vic.gov.au**

## April

### Melbourne International Comedy Festival

The festival, one of the three largest comedy festivals in the world, is held over three and a half weeks in late March and April. The huge program features local and international comedy talent.

Website: **www.comedyfestival.com.au**

## June

### Melbourne International Jazz Festival

First held in 1998, this annual festival is held at venues across the city, both big and small, and highlights the best jazz musicians from Australia and across the world. Website: **www.melbournejazz.com**

## August

### Melbourne International Film Festival

This annual event is a film-lover's paradise screening anticipated new releases as well as classic films over more than two weeks. What could be better than catching up with the latest in film during a Melbourne winter? Website: **www.miff.com.au**

## Melbourne Writers Festival

Bringing together some of the world's leading authors, journalists, playwrights, poets and songwriters in a 10-day celebration of the written word in late August and early September.
Website: **www.mwf.com.au**

# September

## The AFL Grand Final

The AFL (Australian Football League) grand final is traditionally held on the last Saturday in September at the **Melbourne Cricket Ground** (page 68). Even if you're not normally a football fan it's a major event in Melbourne town, so much so that the Friday before is a state public holiday. You need to book tickets months in advance but you could be in any pub in Melbourne and it'll be there on a big TV screen. Website: **www.afl.com.au/tickets/grandfinal**

# October

## Melbourne International Arts Festival

Bringing cutting edge arts performances across all genres to Melbourne from around Australia and the world over 17 days in October. Website: **www.festival.melbourne**

# November

## The Melbourne Cup

What guidebook to Melbourne would be complete without mentioning one of the most famous horse races in the world? This event almost literally stops an entire nation for three and a half minutes but is a public holiday only in Victoria on the first Tuesday in November. As with the AFL Grand Final, you have to book tickets months in advance.

If you do get tickets to Flemington Racecourse on the day – and there are *lots* of package options – be sure to dress up; everyone else will be. It's the one day of the year when you can really show off a hat.

Website: Tickets available through **ticketek.com.au** or **flemington.com.au**

# December

## Moonlight Cinema

Held on the grounds of the **Royal Botanic Gardens** (page 57), the Moonlight Cinema is only open during the warmer months from the end of November to the end of March but is your chance to sit in a park in the evening warmth and watch a movie. You can even take your dog! Website: **www.moonlight.com.au**

## Boxing Day Cricket Test

A highlight of the Australian cricketing calendar, the Boxing Day test match always draws a huge crowd to the MCG.

Website: **www.cricket.com.au**

# Eateries

Obviously, after the considerable exertions involved in enjoying your stay in Melbourne, you're going to have to eat at some point and where and what will depend on your whims, moods and, literally, your tastes.

Naturally, restaurants often change their menus and even their opening times depending on season and time of the year, so we can only offer an approximate idea of highly recommended venues and it's best to check their website for their current status if you're really fussy about what you like to eat.

Any list of 'the best' or 'must haves' is always going to be subjective, and space limitations might mean that we've had to exclude some very worthy establishments, but we've conducted extensive surveys (of our work colleagues and friends) and here are some suggestions for foody experiences that you have to have in Melbourne. In any case, once you're there and have had a chance to ask around you can always chase up other suggestions from the locals.

# Fine Dining

## Attica

74 Glen Eira Road, Ripponlea 3185

Phone: 03 9530 0111

Website: **www.attica.com.au**

Open for dinner 6.00 pm to late Tuesday to Sunday.

Known for: Innovative and constantly acclaimed. Everybody raves about this place. Degustation set menu only. Not far from Ripponlea Station.

## Coda

141 Flinders Lane, Melbourne 3000

Phone: 03 9650 3155

Website: **www.codarestaurant.com.au**

Open for lunch noon to 3.00 pm seven days and for dinner 6.00 pm to late Sunday to Thursday and 5.30 pm to late Friday and Saturday.

Known for: Located in the heart of the city. Modern Vietnamese-French fusion. Bar seating available for patrons without a reservation.

## Cumulus Inc

45 Flinders Lane, Melbourne 3000

Phone: 03 9650 1445

Website: **www.cumulusinc.com.au**

Open seven days from 7.00 am to 11.00 pm Monday to Friday and 8.00 am to 11.00 pm Saturday and Sunday.

Known for: High-end all-day eating in a converted clothing machine shop in the Flinders Lane dining strip.

## Cutler & Co

55–57 Gertrude Street, Fitzroy 3065

Phone: 03 9419 4888

Website: **cutlerandco.com.au**

Open for dinner Tuesday to Saturday from 6.00 pm and all-day
dining from noon on Sunday.

Known for: Sophisticated modern Australian in a converted
metalworks factory with à la carte and degustation options.

## Dans Le Noir?

Rydges Hotel, 701 Swanston Street, Carlton 3053

Phone: 03 9347 7811

Website: **www.melbourne.danslenoir.com**

Open for dinner Thursday to Saturday with arrival between
6.45 pm and 7.45 pm.

Known for: A sensory experience dining in complete darkness,
hosted and served by visually impaired people.

## Epocha

49 Rathdowne Street, Carlton 3053

Phone: 03 9036 4949

Website: **www.epocha.com.au**

Open for lunch Thursday to Sunday from noon to 3.00 pm and for
dinner Monday to Saturday from 5.30 pm till late.

Known for: Modern European overlooking Carlton Gardens in
a beautifully restored terrace building.

## Flower Drum

17 Market Lane, Melbourne 3000

Phone: 03 9662 3655

Website: **www.flowerdrum.melbourne**

Open for lunch Monday to Saturday from noon to 3.00 pm and for dinner Monday to Saturday 6.00 pm to 11.00 pm, Sunday 6.00 pm to 10.30 pm.

Known for: Iconic Chinatown favorite serving Cantonese fine dining (including its signature Peking duck) for more than 30 years.

## Il Bacaro Cucina e Bar

168–170 Little Collins Street, Melbourne 3000

Phone: 03 9654 6778

Website: **www.ilbacaro.com.au**

Open Monday to Saturday for lunch from noon to 3.00 pm and for dinner from 6.00 pm till late.

Known for: Intimate Italian restaurant with a marble-topped bar and starched linen, impeccable service and a huge wine list. Part of the Melbourne restaurant scene for more than 20 years.

## Japanese Teppanyaki-Inn

182 Collins Street, Melbourne 3000

Phone: 03 9650 9432

Website: **www.teppanyaki.com.au**

Open for lunch Tuesday to Friday from noon to 2.00 pm and for dinner Monday to Saturday from 6.00 pm to 10.00 pm.

Known for: Another longstanding Melbourne favorite serving classic Japanese grilled meat and vegetables – it was the first Teppanyaki-style restaurant in Australia.

## Lûmé

226 Coventry Street, South Melbourne 3205

Phone: 03 9690 0185

Website: **www.restaurantlume.com**

Open for lunch Saturday from noon and for dinner Tuesday to Saturday from 6.00 pm.

Known for: Fun dining with progressive and delicious food in a former burlesque club. Multiple tasting menu options available and full vegan and vegetarian menus.

## Maha

21 Bond Street, Melbourne 3000

Phone: 03 9629 5900

Website: **www.maharestaurant.com.au**

Open for lunch and dinner from noon to late seven days.

Known for: An upmarket Middle Eastern sensory experience with Mediterranean/Turkish food by celebrity chef Shane Delia in a contemporary setting. Set menu only with separate vegetarian and vegan menus.

## Minamishima

4 Lord Street, Richmond 3121

Website: **www.minamishima.com.au**

Phone: 03 9429 5180

Open for dinner Tuesday to Saturday from 6.00 pm to 10.00 pm.

Known for: Japanese fine dining in a minimalist room with the option to eat at the sushi bar counter and watch your food being prepared. There are no set or à la carte menus – the chef prepares seasonal sushi options each day and there is matched sake. Reservations essential.

## Philippe

115 Collins Street, Melbourne 3000

Phone: 03 8394 6625

Website: **philipperestaurant.com.au**

Open for lunch Monday to Saturday from noon to 2.30 pm and for dinner Monday to Saturday from 5.30 pm.

Known for: Traditional French restaurant with a contemporary twist and a zinc bar.

## Tonka

20 Duckboard Place, Melbourne 3000

Phone: 03 9650 3155

Website: **www.tonkarestaurant.com.au**

Open for lunch from noon to 3.00 pm and for dinner from 6.00 pm till late seven days.

Known for: Contemporary Indian fine dining in a laneway location with an interesting net art installation on the ceiling and a separate bar menu.

## Vue de Monde

Rialto Towers, 525 Collins Street, Melbourne 3000

Phone: 03 9691 3888

Website: **www.vuedemonde.com.au**

Open for lunch Thursday to Sunday from noon and for dinner from 6.00 pm to 9.00 pm seven days.

Known for: Celebrity chef Shannon Bennett serves up elegant, innovative fine dining. The sweeping city views from the 55th floor of the Rialto building are sensational. Set tasting menu only.

# Gastropubs

'Gastropub' is a word that combines the idea of gastronomy and a pub. They're venues in which the eaties are as important as the drinkies – one up from a cafe but not quite fine dining.

## Builders Arms Hotel

211 Gertrude Street, Fitzroy 3065
Phone: 03 9417 7700
Website: **www.buildersarmshotel.com.au**
Open: Bistro open for lunch Friday to Sunday from noon to 3.30 pm and for dinner Wednesday to Sunday from 5.00 pm to 10.30 pm.
Known for: A landmark pub dating from 1853. Part of chef Andrew McConnell's dining empire so you know the food will be good.

## Fitzroy Town Hall Hotel

166 Johnston Street, Fitzroy 3065
Phone: 03 9416 5055
Website: **www.fitzroytownhallhotel.com.au**
Open: Restaurant open Monday to Wednesday from 3.00 pm till late and Thursday to Sunday from noon till late.
Known for: Seasonal ingredients with European flavors, barbecued meats and a cozy fireplace.

## The Montague

355 Park Street, South Melbourne 3205
Phone: 03 9939 9022
Website: **www.themontague.com.au**
Open noon to late seven days.
Known for: Modern Australian up-market pub favorites.
Not far from **South Melbourne Market** (page 60).

## The Rochester Hotel

182 Johnston Street, Fitzroy 3065

Phone: 03 9419 0166

Website: **www.rochey.com.au**

Open Monday to Wednesday from 2.00 pm to 11.00 pm, Thursday from 2.00 pm to 1.00 am, Friday and Saturday from noon to 3.00 am and Sunday from noon to 11.00 pm.

Known for: The 'Rochey' stands out from other pubs by serving up modern South Indian food, and there's a focus on local wines and craft beers.

## Station Hotel

59 Napier Street, Footscray 3011

Phone: 03 9810 0085

Website: **www.thestationhotel.com.au**

Open noon till late seven days.

Known for: Steaks and French-inspired dining from locally sourced produce. Family friendly.

## Railway Club Hotel

107 Raglan Street, Port Melbourne 3207

Phone: 03 9645 1661

Website: **www.railwayclubhotel.com.au**

Open Monday to Saturday 11.00 am to 12.00 am, Sunday 11.00 am to 11.00 pm.

Known for: Renowned for its reasonably priced grass-fed beef in a buzzy dining room.

# Sweet Stuff – Cafe Patisseries

## Brunetti Carlton

Lygon Court, 380 Lygon Street, Carlton 3053

Phone: 03 9347 2801

Website: **www.brunetti.com.au**

Open 6.00 am to 10.00 pm Sunday to Thursday and 6.00 am to 11.00 pm Friday and Saturday.

Known for: A Melbourne icon, it doesn't stop at cake; it also does pizza and gelato. Brunetti also has outlets in Flinders Lane and Myer Melbourne in the city and at Melbourne Airport.

## The French Lettuce

237 Nicholson Street, Carlton 3053

Phone: 03 9347 7105

Website: **www.thefrenchlettuce.com**

Open 9.00 am to 5.00 pm Monday, 7.00 am to 5.00 pm Tuesday to Saturday and 7.00 am to 3.00 pm Sunday.

Known for: An institution that has been operating for 35 years, the window displays are stunning and the wedding cakes extraordinary.

## ST. ALi

12–18 Yarra Place, South Melbourne 3205

Phone: 03 9686 2990

Website: **www.stali.com.au**

Open 7.00 am to 6.00 pm seven days.

Known for: A hipster coffee pioneer with specialty coffee techniques like pour over and syphon. Located in a converted warehouse and also known for its inventive brunches.

## Le Bon Continental Cake Shop

93 Acland Street, St Kilda 3182
Phone: 03 9534 2515
Open 8.00 am to 11.00 pm seven days.
Known for: Acland Street is known for its traditional cake shops
with their tempting and irresistible window displays and Le Bon
has been around for more than 40 years.

## Monarch Cakes

103 Acland Street, St Kilda 3182
Phone: 03 9534 2972
Website: **www.monarchcakes.com.au**
Open 8.00 am to 10.00 pm seven days.
Known for: Operating in Acland Street since 1934, Monarch Cakes
was founded by Polish immigrants and focuses on Eastern
European favorites like kouglhoupf, poppy seed cake, strudel
and baked cheesecake.

## Afternoon Tea at the Hotel Winsor

111 Spring Street, Melbourne 3000
Phone: 03 9633 6000
Website: **www.thehotelwindsor.com.au/afternoontea**
Open: 11.30 am to 2.00 pm Monday and Tuesday, 11.30 am to
4.30 pm Wednesday to Sunday.
Known for: If you want just that little bit of extra luxury, without
going too crazy, there's nothing quite as elegant as high tea
in a swanky hotel. You really need to look at the website, as
there are a number of different afternoon tea options, they vary
seasonally, and there are specials too.

# Simply the Best

## The Best Basque – Naked for Satan

285 Brunswick Street, Fitzroy 3065

Phone: 03 9416 2238

Website: **www.nakedforsatan.com.au**

Open noon to 12.00 am Sunday to Thursday, noon to 1.00 am
  Friday and Saturday.

Because how often do you get to eat Basque food?

## The Best Dumplings – I Love Dumplings

30A Breese Street, Brunswick 3056

Phone: 03 9386 3868

297 Racecourse Road, Flemington/Kensington 3031

Phone: 03 9372 5218

298 Bridge Rd, Richmond 3121

Phone: 03 9428 9201

2/29 Fitzroy Street, St Kilda 3182

Phone: 03 9078 5414

Website: **www.ilovedumpling.com.au**

Open Individual store hours vary but generally from 11.30 am to
  3.00 pm and 5.00 pm to 9.00 pm seven days.

## The Best Grill – San Telmo Argentinean Grill

14 Meyers Place, Melbourne 3000

Phone: 03 9650 5525

Website: **www.santelmo.com.au**

Open noon to 11.00 pm seven days.

### The Best Korean Food – Mahn Doo

365 La Trobe Street, Melbourne 3000
Phone: 03 9606 0017
Website: **www.mahndoo.com**
Open for lunch noon to 2.30 pm Monday to Friday and for dinner
  5.30 pm to 10.00 pm Monday to Saturday.

### The Best Laksa – Laksa King Flemington

6–16 Pin Oak Crescent, Flemington 3031
Phone: 03 9372 6383
Website: **www.laksaking.com.au**

### The Best Pizza – 400 Gradi

99 Lygon Street, Brunswick East 3057
Phone: 03 9380 2320
Crown Casino, 8 Whiteman Street, Southbank 3006
Phone: 03 9292 5777
Website: **www.400gradi.com.au**
Open noon to 11.00 pm seven days.

### The Best Spanish Food – Robert Burns Hotel

376 Smith Street, Collingwood 3066
Phone: 03 9417 2233
Website: **www.robertburnshotel.com.au**
Open noon to 12.00 am Monday to Saturday and noon to
  11.00 pm Sunday.

## The Best Vegetarian – Lentil as Anything

1/3 St Helliers Street, Abbotsford 3067
(part of the **Abbotsford Convent** complex (page 90))
Phone: 03 9419 6444
41 Blessington Street, St Kilda 3182
Phone: 0424 345 368
Website: www.lentilasanything.com
Open Abbotsford open for breakfast from 9.00 am to 11.30 am,
   for lunch from noon to 4.00 pm and for dinner from 5.30 pm
   to 9.00 pm seven days. St Kilda open for lunch from noon to
   5.00 pm and for dinner from 5.30 pm to 9.00 pm seven days.
It's run entirely by volunteers and you pay by donation – however
much you like and however generous you want to be. Extraordinary!

## The Best Vietnamese Pork Rolls – Trang Bakery and Cafe

382 Smith Street, Collingwood 3066
Phone: 03 9722 4352
Open 8.00 am to 5.00 pm seven days.
There's always a queue at peak times. A vegan menu is available and
there are other outlets at Albert Park, South Yarra and Camberwell.

# Drinkeries

Enjoying Melbourne can be dehydrating, so you'll want to sit down for a drink at some point. Some of these places are a little out of the way, but they give you an opportunity to explore the city beyond its center and maybe mix a little with the locals.

In case the message hasn't gotten through yet, Melbourne is a city of bars and pubs (and, of course, **cafes** page 141). Space prohibits an exhaustive list of venues but here are some of those most worthy of note.

## Hidden Bars

If you like that out-of-the-main-drag, exclusive feel – some are so exclusive they don't even reveal their phone numbers. We won't tell you how to get there, searching for them is half the fun.

### *The Croft Institute*

21 Croft Alley, Melbourne 3000
Phone: 03 9671 4399
Website: **www.thecroftinstitute.com.au**
Open 5.00 pm to 1.00 am Monday to Thursday, 5.00 pm to 3.00 am Friday, 8.00 pm to 3.00 am Saturday.
Known for: Located in a Chinatown alley, it looks like an old-school science lab and has DJs on Friday and Saturday nights.

## Goldilocks Bar

264 Swanston Street, Melbourne 3000

Website: **www.goldilocksbar.com**

Open 4.00 pm till late Monday to Wednesday, 2.00 pm to 1.00 am Thursday to Sunday.

Known for: Rooftop bar with city views and a menu that includes lots of vegetarian and vegan options. The drinks focus on local and sustainable beer, cider and wine.

## Loch & Key

34 Franklin Street, Melbourne 3000

Phone: 0408 140 043

Website: **www.lochandkey.com.au**

Open 5.00 pm to 5.00 am Sunday to Thursday, 4.00 pm to 7.00 am Friday, 5.00 pm to 7.00 am Saturday.

Known for: Hidden up a rickety staircase this dark wood bar features private booths and a balcony terrace with city views.

## Rooftop at QT

11/133 Russell Street, Melbourne 3000

Phone: 03 8636 8800

Website: **www.qthotelsandresorts.com/melbourne/eat-drink**

Open noon till late Monday to Friday, 2.00 pm till late Saturday and Sunday.

Known for: The glamorous decor, spectacular city views and the dress code that attracts a sophisticated crowd. If you prefer your drink with a view there's also **Rooftop Bar at Curtin House** (page 125) with a truly impressive view at night! Phone: 03 9654 5394; Website: **www.rooftopbar.co**.

# Laneway Bars

Melbourne is gifted with a number of great laneway bars (some of which are pretty well hidden and exclusive too). Visiting these bars is a perfect pretext for exploring Melbourne's little streets and seeing what else you'll find there.

## *Arlechin*

Mornane Place, Melbourne 3000

Website: **www.arlechin.com.au**

Open 5.00 pm to 3.00 am Wednesday to Sunday.

Known for: Stylish cocktail and wine bar by acclaimed Italian chef Guy Grossi (**Florentino**) with interesting Italian-influenced bar food.

## *Bar Americano*

20 Presgrave Place, Melbourne 3000

Website: **www.baramericano.com**

Open 5.00 pm till sold out Monday, 5.00 pm till 11.00 pm Tuesday and Wednesday, 5.00 pm till midnight Thursday to Saturday.

Known for: Standing room only, the tiny room is inspired by American bars of the Prohibition era and Italian standup espresso bars. Serving classic cocktails, they take cards only – no cash.

## Bar Tini

3–5 Hosier Lane, Melbourne 3000

Phone 03 9663 3038

Website: **www.bartini.com.au**

Open 5.00 pm to 11.00 pm Tuesday and Wednesday, 5.00 pm to 12.00 am Thursday, 5.00 pm to 1.00 am Friday and Saturday.

Known for: Owned by the team behind the ever-popular Movida Spanish restaurant, Bar Tini sells top-quality Spanish tinned fish and other delicious Spanish bites and there's an extensive wine list. Located in Hosier Lane that attracts the crowds for its graffitied walls.

## Eau de Vie – EDV

1 Malthouse Lane, Melbourne 3000

Phone: 03 8393 9367

Website: **www.eaudevie.com.au**

Open 5.00 pm to 1.00 am Monday to Thursday, 4.00 pm to 1.00 am Friday to Sunday.

Known for: Glamorous bar inspired by Prohibition-era America with a focus on whiskey (there are hundreds of them!), cocktails, jazz music and a full upmarket dining menu.

## Gin Palace

10 Russell Place, Melbourne 3000

Phone: 03 9654 0533

Website: **www.ginpalace.com.au**

Open 4.00 pm to 3.00 am seven days.

Known for: Dark, plush, upmarket bar known for martinis and gin-based cocktails.

## Murmur Piano Bar

17 Warburton Lane, Melbourne 3000

Website: **www.murmur.com.au**

Phone: 03 9640 0395

Open 4.30 pm till late Tuesday to Saturday.

Known for: Live piano music by the house pianist, and delicious Spanish tapas.

## Section 8

27–29 Tattersalls Lane, Melbourne 3000

Phone: 0430 291 588

Website: **www.section8.com.au**

Open noon to 11.00 pm Sunday, 10.00 am to 11.00 pm Monday to Wednesday, 10.00 am to 1.00 am Thursday and Friday, noon to 1.00 am Saturday.

Known for: Funky, hipster bar in a shipping container in a graffitied parking lot in Chinatown with recycled wooden pallets for seating. Imported beers and great cocktails.

## Union Electric Bar & Rooftop Gin Garden

13 Heffernan Lane, Melbourne VIC 3000

Phone 0450 186 466

Website: **www.unionelectric.com.au**

Open: 5.00 pm to 12.00 am daily.

Known for: Casual bar with fun fruity cocktails, indoor and outdoor seating and BYO food!

# Pubs

Back in the olden days premises that were licensed for the sale of alcohol were divided into private bars, located within private clubs of which you had to be a member, and pubs (public bars), which were open to the general public. Since then, we've come a long way and 'pub' can mean anything from old-timey local watering holes to sophisticated, family-friendly establishments which serve food just short of fine dining.

Unlike bars, Melbourne pubs are usually open seven days, usually from about 11.00 am to 11.00 pm or longer, but ring ahead to check as, in so many other things, pub opening times in Melbourne can be seasonal. Also, unlike bars, pubs usually don't make a virtue of exclusivity so they're usually as welcoming as they can be.

The list of Melbourne's top pubs is arguable, but the ones mentioned below are among the favorites in the opinion of many.

## The Top Pubs

### North Melbourne Town Hall

33 Errol Street, North Melbourne 3051
Phone: 03 9328 1983
Website: **www.townhallhotelnorthmelbourne.com.au**
Open 4.00 pm to 1.00 am Monday to Thursday, noon to 1.00 am Friday and Saturday, noon to 11.00 pm Sunday.
Known for: Iconic working-class pub with live music and cheap eats, a beer garden and fireplace for the colder months.

## The Drunken Poet

65 Peel Street, West Melbourne 3003

Phone: 03 9348 9797

Website: **www.thedrunkenpoet.com.au**

Open noon to 1.00 am Tuesday to Saturday, noon to 11.00 pm
  Sunday.

Known for: Irish pub with live music six nights a week.
  It's right next to **Queen Victoria Markets** (page 55)

## The Great Northern Hotel

644 Rathdowne Street, Carlton North 3054

Phone: 03 9380 9569

Website: **www.gnh.net.au**

Open 11.00 am till midnight Monday to Thursday, 11.00 am till
  1.00 am Friday and Saturday, 11.00 am till 11.00 pm Sunday.

Known for: The large beer garden, an incredible 21 beer taps with
  a passion for craft beer. Dogs encouraged!

## The Hotel Esplanade

11 The Esplanade, St Kilda 3182

Phone: 03 9534 0211

Website: **www.hotelesplanade.com.au**

Open 12.00 pm till late Monday to Thursday, 11.00 am till late
  Friday to Sunday.

Known for: A Melbourne institution, known as 'The Espy', it was
  built as a resort hotel in 1878. Famous for live music, the TV
  music quiz show *Rockwiz* was filmed here. The Espy has
  had several owners over the last decade and controversial
  redevelopment plans, with renovations taking place in 2018.
  There are still 3 stages for live music, 12 bars and 2 restaurants

## The Mount View Hotel

68/70 Bridge Road, Richmond 3121

Phone: 03 9428 3973

Website: **www.mtviewhotel.com.au**

Open noon to 11.00 pm Sunday to Thursday, noon to 1.00 am Friday and Saturday.

Known for: A sports pub close to the MCG with craft beers and cocktails, rooftop bar with amazing city views and a menu of quality pub classics.

## The Standard Hotel

293 Fitzroy Street, Fitzroy 3065

Phone: 03 9419 4793

Website: **www.thestandardhotel.com.au**

Open 3.00 pm to 10.00 pm Monday, 3.00 pm to 11.00 pm Tuesday, noon to 11.00 pm Wednesday to Saturday, noon to 10.00 pm Sunday.

Known for: Character-filled historic pub with a lovely leafy beer garden.

# Fireplace Pubs

Melbourne can get cold, especially in the winter (or for anything from five minutes to all day at any other time of the year!). It might be an idea to settle in front of a fire.

## *Marquis of Lorne*

411 George Street, Fitzroy 3065
Phone: 03 9417 5001
Website: **www.marquisoflorne.com.au**
Open 4.00 pm to 11.00 pm Monday to Wednesday, noon to
  1.00 am Thursday to Saturday, noon to 11.00 pm Sunday.
Known for: Charming old pub with interesting, quality pub food
  with a focus on meat. There's a rooftop area for the warmer
  months too!

## *The Local Taphouse*

184 Carlisle Street, East St Kilda 3183
Phone: 03 9537 2633
Website: **www.thelocal.com.au**
Open noon till late Sunday to Thursday, noon to 1.00 am Friday
  and Saturday.
Known for: Stylish, European-inspired bar specializing in craft beer
  with upmarket food options, a cozy downstairs bar and rooftop
  courtyard. Also hosts a comedy night.

## The Napier Hotel

210 Napier Street, Fitzroy 3065

Phone: 03 9419 4240

Website: **www.thenapierhotel.com**

Open 3.00 pm to 11.00 pm Monday to Thursday, noon to 1.00 am Friday, noon to 11.00 pm Saturday and 1.00 pm to 11.00 pm Sunday.

Known for: Warm and inviting with a pool lounge, courtyard and upmarket but well-priced food including vegan options.

## The Union Club Hotel

164 Gore Street, Fitzroy 3065

Phone: 03 9417 2926

Website: **www.unionclubhotel.com.au**

Open 3.00 pm till late Monday to Wednesday, noon till late Thursday to Saturday, noon to 11.00 pm Sunday.

Known for: Local hipster pub with shabby-chic vintage decor, a leafy undercover beer garden and a menu of quality pub classics.

## Live Music Pubs

## Bendigo Hotel

125 Johnston Street, Collingwood 3066

Phone: 03 9417 3415

Website: **www.bendigohotel.com.au**

Open 4.00 pm till late Monday, Wednesday and Thursday, 3.00 pm to 3.00 am Friday and Saturday, 3.00 pm to 11.30 pm Sunday.

Known for: Live music Tuesday to Sunday with a focus on heavy metal.

## Northcote Social

301 High Street, Northcote 3070

Phone: 03 9489 3917

Website: **www.northcotesocialclub.com**

Open 4.00 pm till late Monday, noon till late Tuesday to Sunday.

Known for: Hipster bar with up-and-coming indie music acts, an upmarket pub menu with lots of vegetarian, vegan and gluten free options and a big, heated deck.

## Retreat Hotel

280 Sydney Road, Brunswick 3056

Phone: 03 9380 4090

Website: **www.retreathotelbrunswick.com.au**

Open noon to 1.00 am Sunday to Thursday, noon to 3.00 am Friday and Saturday.

Known for: A wide range of live music including jazz, funk and soul in a bar with charming original decor and a menu with plenty of vegetarian and gluten-free options.

## The Corner Hotel

57 Swan Street, Richmond 3121

Phone: 03 9427 7300

Website: **www.cornerhotel.com**

Open noon till late Sunday to Thursday, noon to 3.00 am Friday and Saturday.

Known for: One of Melbourne's most celebrated live music venues with a room that can take 800 people and has hosted some of the world's biggest names.

## The Gem

289 Wellington Street, Collingwood 3066

Phone: 03 9419 5170

Website: **www.thegembar.com.au**

Open 3.00 pm to 11.00 pm Tuesday to Thursday, noon to 1.00 am
Friday and Saturday, noon to 11.00 pm Sunday.

Known for: Wood-paneled hipster Americana bar with a shrine
to Elvis Presley and a Texas barbecue menu with vegetarian
options. Musicians and DJs perform Friday to Sunday.
Frozen margaritas available in summer.

## The Tote

67–71 Johnston Street, Collingwood 3066

Phone: 03 9419 5320

Website: **www.thetotehotel.com**

Open 4.00 pm to 1.00 am Wednesday, 4.00 pm to 3.00 am
Thursday to Saturday, 4.00 pm to 11.00 pm Sunday.

Known for: Legendary venue for punk and psychedelic rock bands.

# Breweries

Here are the best breweries in the CBD.

## Colonial Brewing Co

89 Bertie Street, Port Melbourne 3207

Phone: 03 8644 4044

Website: **www.colonialbrewingco.com.au/port-melbourne**

Open noon to 6.00 pm Thursday and Sunday, 11.00 am till late
Friday, noon till late Saturday.

Known for: Not far from **Southbank** (page 126), with burgers,
pizzas, music and beer, of course!

## Moon Dog Brewery Bar

17 Duke Street, Abbotsford 3067

Phone: 03 9428 2307

Website: **www.moondogbrewing.com.au**

Open 4.00 pm to 11.00 pm Tuesday to Friday, noon to 11.00 pm
Saturday, noon to 8.00 pm Sunday.

Known for: Located in a light industrial area, the funky brewery bar
has comfy couches, palm trees and a pizza van.

## Mountain Goat Beer

80 North Street, Richmond 3121

Phone: 03 9428 1180

Website: **www.goatbeer.com.au**

Open 5.00 pm to 10.00 pm Wednesday, 5.00 pm to 11.00 pm
Fridays, noon to 6.00 pm Sunday.

Known for: Special release beers on tap, pizzas with vegetarian,
vegan and gluten free options.

## Temple Brewery Company

122 Weston Street, Brunswick East 3057

Phone: 03 9380 8999

Website: **www.templebrewing.com.au**

Open 5.00 pm to 11.00 pm Thursday, noon to 11.00 pm Friday
and Saturday, noon to 9.00 pm Sunday.

Known for: The funky, pet-friendly Brewhouse Bar serving up
delicious food. Not far from **Melbourne Zoo** (page 53).

## The Craft & Co

390 Smith Street, Collingwood 3066

Phone: 03 9417 4755

Website: **www.thecraftandco.com.au**

Open 10.00 am to 10.00 pm Wednesday and Thursday, 10.00 am to 11.00 pm Friday and Saturday, 10.00 am to 6.00 pm Sunday.

Known for: They do it all – brewery, distillery, winery, eatery and micro-dairy! A range of food options including the housemade cheese.

## Thunder Road Brewery

130 Barkly Street Brunswick 3056

Phone: **www.thunderroadbrewing.com**

Website: 1800 831 817

Open 4.00 pm to 11.00 pm Friday, noon to 11.00 pm Saturday, noon to 9.00 pm Sunday.

Known for: There is a large sunny courtyard with food served from an Airstream caravan. Not far from **Melbourne Zoo** (page 53).

## Aussie Brewery Tours

For those who simply can't get enough of the fermented amber liquids you might consider going on a beer tour. Prices start from $89 per person for the **Red Hill Brewery Tour** that will take you to the Mornington Peninsula, to the $105 **Melbourne Urban Night Tour**, to the **Mornington Peninsula Cider and Beer Adventure**, **The Melbourne Beer Odyssey** and the **Yarra Valley Cider and Ale Trail** all $160 per person, the Brew Your Own Ale Tour for $212 and much, much more.

Phone: 1300 787 039; Website: **www.aussiebrewerytours.com.au**

First published in 2019 by New Holland Publishers
Sydney • Auckland

Level 1, 178 Fox Valley Road, Wahroonga, NSW 2076, Australia
5/39 Woodside Ave, Northcote, Auckland 0627, New Zealand

newhollandpublishers.com

A record of this book is held at the National Library of Australia.

ISBN 9781760791391

Group Managing Director: Fiona Schultz
Author: Xavier Waterkeyn
Project Editor: Liz Hardy
Designer: Andrew Davies
Production Director: Arlene Gippert
Printer: Toppan Leefung Printing Limited

10 9 8 7 6 5 4 3 2 1

Keep up with New Holland Publishers:
 NewHollandPublishers
 @newhollandpublishers

Page 1: The iconic bathing boxes of Brighton Beach.